THE AGING EMPLOYEE

G P 8700948

THE AGING EMPLOYEE

Edited by

Stanley F. Yolles, M.D.

*State University of New York
at Stony Brook
Stony Brook, New York*

Leonard W. Krinsky, Ph.D.

*South Oaks Hospital
Amityville, New York*

Sherman N. Kieffer, M.D.

*State University of New York
at Stony Brook
Stony Brook, New York*

Pasquale A. Carone, M.D.

*South Oaks Hospital
Amityville, New York*

**Volume VIII: Problems of Industrial Psychiatric
Medicine Series**
Series Editor: Sherman N. Kieffer, M.D.

HUMAN SCIENCES PRESS, INC.
72 FIFTH AVENUE
NEW YORK, N.Y. 10011

Printed in the United States of America
123456789

Library of Congress Cataloging in Publication Data
Main entry under title:

The Aging employee.

(Problems of industrial psychiatric medicine series, ISSN 0277-4178; v. 8)
Procceedings of a conference entitled "Mental health and industry—a look at the aging employee," held on April 10-11, 1980, sponsored by South Oaks Foundation and the Dept. of Psychiatry, Health Sciences Center, State Univ. of N.Y. at Stony Brook.
Includes index.
1. Age and employment—Congresses. I. Yolles, Stanley F., 1919-   II. South Oaks Foundation.
III. State University of New York at Stony Brook.

Library of Congress Cataloging in Publication Data

IV. Series: Problems of industrial psychiatric medicine; v. 8. Dept. of Psychiatry.
HD6279.A36 1984   331.3 '94 '0973   83-285
ISBN 0-89885-106-8

CONTENTS

ACKNOWLEDGMENTS

A book such as this requires very active involvement and cooperation on the part of a number of different groups. The speakers and
panelists not only had to involve themselves actively in the conference
which brought this book forth, but also had to spend a great deal of
time and effort in working with typescripts to further clarify and en-
rich their statements. Each of our speakers and panelists made individual contributions both at the meeting and to the editing of this
volume.

The Board of Directors of South Oaks Hospital has actively backed
the Foundation and the conference over the years. We are deeply in-
debted to them for the commitment they have always offered in
attacking the problems of psychiatric medicine.

Our acknowledgments would be incomplete without mentioning
the tremendous help of our executive assistant, Catherine Martens,
and our director of community relations, Lynn Black.

This volume is one in which proponents of varying viewpoints had
an opportunity to come together for a synthesis of opinions. Certain
definitive findings were established, and indications suggested which
undoubtedly will lead to further discussions. A major benefit was the
bringing together of representatives of diverse groups so that a
common denominator for working together could be found.

CONTRIBUTORS

JOSEPH S. BARBARO, C.S.W.
Executive Director
Catholic Charities
Diocese of Rockville Centre

JEROME L. BLAUNSTEIN, M.D.
Area Medical Director
AT&T Long Lines

WILLIAM BOLCH
President
Local 32293
Mutual Ticket Agents Union

PENNY WISE BUDOFF, M.D.
Assistant Professor of Clinical Family
    Medicine
Health Sciences Center
State University of New York at
    Stony Brook

PASQUALE A. CARONE, M.D.
Executive Director
South Oaks Hospital, and Director
South Oaks Foundation

9

FREDERICK B.E. CHARATAN, M.D.
Chief of Psychiatry
Jewish Institute for Geriatric Care
Long Island Jewish/Hillside Medical
  Center

ROSE LAUB COSER, Ph.D.
Professor of Community and
  Preventive Medicine
School of Medicine, Health Sciences
  Center
State University of New York at
  Stony Brook

FRANCES S. DOWDY, R.N.
Director of Nursing
Broadlawn Manor Nursing Home
  and Health-Related Facility

LEON HANKOFF, M.D.
Professor of Psychiatry
Department of Psychiatry and
  Behavioral Science
School of Medicine
Health Sciences Center
State University of New York at
  Stony Brook

AUDREY H. JONES
Personnel Policies and Services
Manager
Long Island Lighting Company

STUART L. KEILL, M.D.
Clinical Professor and Vice
Chairman
Department of Psychiatry
State University of New York at
Buffalo

10

SHERMAN N. KIEFFER, M.D.
Professor and Vice Chairman
Department of Psychiatry and
    Behavioral Science
School of Medicine
Health Sciences Center
State University of New York at
    Stony Brook

DANIEL E. KNOWLES
Director of Personnel
Grumman Aerospace Corporation

PETER KRAJESKI
Director of Personnel
South Oaks Hospital

LEONARD W. KRINKSY, Ph.D.
Administrator and Director of
    Psychological Services
South Oaks Hospital

ELEANOR LITWAK
Director
DC-37 Educational and Cultural Program
American Federation of State, County, and
    Municipal Employees

JOHN J. McMANUS
Assistant Director
Department of Community Services
AFL/CIO, Washington, D.C.

JAMES E. RAMSEUR, M.A.
Director
Central Islip Psychiatric Center

JULIAN SCHWARTZ, M.D.
Consultant

11

Internal Medicine and
  Gastroenterology
South Oaks Hospital

Isidore Shapiro, A.C.S.W.
Commissioner
Nassau County Department of
  Mental Health

Alexander Stieglitz
Executive Chairman
Air Transport Lodge 1056
International Association of Machinists and
  Aerospace Workers

Sivachandra M. Vallury, M.D.
Senior Psychiatrist
South Oaks Hospital

Peter Van Putten, Jr.
Director of Personnel
Hazeltine Corporation

William Voorhest
Special Assistant to the President
Grumman Aerospace Corporation

Morton Ward, M.D.
Medical Director
Philadelphia Geriatric Center

Charles Winick
Consultant
Central Labor Rehabilitation
Council of New York

Stanley F. Yolles, M.D.
Professor and Chairman

12

Department of Psychiatry and
  Behavioral Science
School of Medicine, Health Sciences
  Center
State University of New York at
  Stony Brook

RICHARD M. ZOPPA, M.D.
Senior Psychiatrist
South Oaks Hospital

PREFACE

The present volume is the eighth relating to problems of industrial psychiatric medicine. South Oaks Foundation in conjunction with the Department of Psychiatry, Health Sciences Center, State University of New York at Stony Brook has been involved for a number years in sponsoring conferences which afford a forum where representatives of psychiatry, psychology, and social work meet in collaborative efforts with representatives of labor, management, and government.

Our first conference, entitled "Alcoholism in Industry," was held in 1971, and we have since had conferences on "Drug Abuse in Industry," "Women in Industry," and "Absenteeism in Industry," among others.

On April 10th and 11th, 1980, we held a conference entitled "Mental Health and Industry—A Look at the Aging Employee." The problem of the aging employee must be differentiated from that of the problems of retirement. The aging employee is actively involved on the job and is an extremely valuable worker, and efforts must be exerted to maintain his or her efficiency. In the case of the retired employee, he or she has already left the work situation and has an entirely different set of problems which we have addressed in a previous conference. In this volume, experts in various fields have discussed the advantages and disadvantages connected with the aging employee.

INTRODUCTION

This book is concerned with bringing together members of various disciplines to confront the problem of the aging employee. It is our hope that by having representatives of the mental health professions, psychiatry, psychology, and social work meet with representatives of labor, management, and government that we can face meaningfully into a problem area that is already present and will continue to grow in importance. As the life span of our citizens lengthens, and as laws are changed which permit deferring retirement, more and more of our labor force will be in the older age group. We live in a society where the cult of youth is worshipped. Media and advertising hype bombard us with the glossy images of the young and the beautiful. To be young is good. To be older, by inference, is bad.

For anyone over the "old" age of 40, this begins to bring about the self-fulfilling prophecy—especially in the workplace. Because management's expectations are that the usefulness and value of these employees are diminishing, the employees begin to perceive themselves in the same way. It is an insidious process. Myths and stereotypes about middle-aged and older employees become ingrained in the perceptions of both management and employee. It is time we looked at the many studies which have shown that there are no significant differences in job performance and absenteeism between the younger and older employees. We must begin to question the myths and stereotypes.

The various contributors to this volume offer thoughts and opinions as to these myths and stereotypes:

It is to be expected that more and more people will defer retirement, and not only at present, but in the future, we can expect an older employee population than we have had in the past. This should not only result in greater efficiency in that the workers are already trained and have a proven history of being responsible and dedicated, but there are obviously problems that inevitably must arise as older employees remain on the job. Certainly this places the older worker on some sort of collision course with a society which figuratively worships the cult of youth.

The middle-aged and older worker represent the largest of the so-called "minority groups" in the United States' work force. The most insidious type of discrimination is subconscious and subtle; age discrimination is insidious because it is perpetuated by other older workers; and since the middle-aged and older workers are the largest of the so-called protected groups, more cases of discrimination probably take place against them on the sheer weight of statistics.

The quality of life and the aging worker are, after all not incompatible partners, are not insurmountable as barriers, and do not necessarily have to separate at the chronological age benchmarks of 36, 45, 55, or 75 or 150. Professional medicine has kept us living longer and at the same time technology has made us increasingly obsolete.

Their conclusions are clear. The challenge is a growing one. The labor force is growing older. Older workers are more reliable, are more ego-involved and have less absenteeism. Use of illicit drugs is not a problem, but alcohol is. A greater involvement in decision-making and more active participation by workers and what happens to them in the company is more important with the older worker than it is with the younger. Pre-retirement counseling is a necessity with our aging employee.

The purpose of this conference was to educate, and to establish lines of communication. We see this conference not as an end but really as a beginning, as the first of what we hope will be many conferences directed toward the special area of the aging employee.

Chapter 1

SOME COMMON PSYCHIATRIC PROBLEMS OF AGING EMPLOYEES

Fred B. Charatan, M.D. *

Aging employees are distinguished by a number of desirable occupational characteristics. They have settled habits and attitudes. They have a sense of responsibility, reliability, and conscientiousness. They maintain interest in their job. They demonstrate willingness to give a fair day's work for a fair day's pay. They are loyal and cooperative. They are less argumentative and aggressive than younger employees, although perhaps more inclined to resist advice and

---

*Dr. Charatan, a native of London, England, received his medical training at St. Thomas's Hospital Medical School. He later trained in psychiatry at the Maudsley Hospital, London. He came to New York in 1957, and did research on tranquilizers at Manhattan State Hospital. From 1966 to 1972 he was Mental Health Director for Nassau County, New York. Since 1972, he has been Chief of Psychiatry, Jewish Institute for Geriatric Care, and Attending Psychiatrist, Long Island Jewish-Hillside Medical Center.

Dr. Charatan is Associate Professor of Clinical Psychiatry, School of Medicine, Health Sciences Center, State University of New York at Stony Brook. He is a Fellow of the American Psychiatric Association, a Member of the Gerontological Society, and Consulting Editor of **Hospital Physician** and **Gerontology and Geriatrics Education**. He has published over 40 articles in American and British journals, mostly in geriatric psychiatry.

instruction. Finally, they are less accident-prone because they are more careful and experienced.[1]

Older workers are in a more vulnerable position than younger ones, since they cannot find new jobs easily. They are also less mobile. It is obviously in their own interest to retain their jobs, work efficiently, and maintain an unblemished record. The aging employee will have established his or her performance over many years, and views an honorable retirement and well-earned pension as goals worth striving for. At the same time, the aging employee is susceptible to some common psychiatric problems which, at this phase of the life cycle, have certain distinguishing features. It is traditional to designate these as functional or organic, although in practice one cannot always separate the two.

PSYCHONEUROSES IN AGING EMPLOYEES

Anxiety in aging employees may be free-floating, or it may be expressed in somatic symptoms such as tension, tremors, perspiration, hyperventilation, rapid heart rate, forgetfulness, insomnia or unrefreshing sleep, and anorexia. The subject looks worried and preoccupied, and may have painful ruminations or worrying thoughts about his job performance and effectiveness.

The anxiety in these subjects, as at other ages, may give rise to phobic reactions with or without panic attacks, or may take the form of an obsessive-compulsive disorder. Here, the employee is likely to caricature so-called normal behavior with increasingly inflexible uniformity in job operations, over-rigidity, repeated checking and counterchecking, and excessive self-doubt and criticism. The longer he stays at his desk or bench, the less he achieves.

The genesis of anxiety in the older person is the actual, threatened, or fantasied experience of depletion. With aging, psychological and physical reserves are progressively depleted. Like in the very young, aging persons often fear loss or separation. They are afraid that their declining powers may not prove adequate to what they themselves and their superiors expect of their performance. Ernest Hemingway said, at the age of 53, "As you get older it is harder to have heroes, but it is sort of necessary." Anxiety over sexual adequacy, so characteristic of the earlier period of life, tends to be replaced by anxiety about job performance.

Yet another important area of anxiety is the transition from work to retirement.[2] Depending upon the subject's attitude, retirement can represent relegation to the scrap heap, or a prolonged and blissful vacation. The critical phase for adjustment is the period before retirement. It is during this time that workers become increasingly agitated about the possible consequences and problems.

Finally, because aging is so often accompanied by an increase in degenerative conditions which do not necessarily reach the level of clinical illness, many aging employees become preoccupied with their bodies, and even hypochrondriacal. This results in anxiety, and perhaps in recourse to over-the-counter medications, dietary regimens, and quack rejuvenation courses. Older employees visit their physicians more frequently than the young, seeking relief for symptoms which are often vague and difficult to evaluate. Where somatic symptoms are more a reflection of hypochondriacal anxiety than established somatic disease, the work performance of the aging employee may be seriously affected, and frequent absenteeism may compromise his effectiveness.

ALCOHOLISM

Psychoneurotic anxiety may lead to alcohol abuse. In the aging employee, recourse to alcohol often represents an attempt at self-medication to relieve anxiety not resolvable by other means. The older alcoholic is not necessarily the younger alcoholic grown old. Zimbert (1974)[3] pointed out that at least one-third of older alcoholics in San Francisco had begun abusing alcohol after age 60. Older alcoholics are more likely to be heavy smokers, to report serious health difficulties, and to have a higher rate of organic brain syndrome. The average elderly alcoholic, it should be emphasized, is not a skid-row denizen, but a blue-collar or white-collar worker with many strengths apart from the alcohol problem. This type of drinker is more likely to be living alone, is depressed, shows social instability (moving domicile frequently), and has a reduced physical reserve often arising from chronic lung disease due to the associated heavy smoking. Poor nutrition is also a common complicating factor.[4]

A most important correlate of alcohol abuse in the older employee is a relatively high rate of attempted suicide. The suicide rate in elderly white males rises to three times the national rate. Alcoholism is frequently associated with completed suicide in this age group.

AFFECTIVE DISORDERS

The commonest functional mental disorder of aging employees is undoubtedly depression. Approximately one-third of persons over the age of 60 have depressive symptoms, and it seems that depression is relatively underdiagnosed in the elderly. The criteria for a diagnosis of depression have been embodied in the Diagnostic and Statistical Manual III of the American Psychiatric Association.[5] The criteria are:

1. Dysphoric depressive mood manifested by sadness, hopelessness, feeling low, discouraged, "blue," empty and without feeling, worried, weepiness and irritability.

2. Poor appetite, or weight loss of more than one pound per week when not dieting.

3. Alteration of sleep pattern. Insomnia, especially with frequent wakings during the night or early in the morning, not solely due to need to urinate, with difficulty in returning to sleep, is present in agitated depression. Increased sleep, often with difficulty in getting up in the morning, is seen in retarded depression.

4. Loss of subjective energy or easy fatigability.

5. Objective psychomotor agitation or retardation.

6. Difficulty in concentration or thinking, i.e., inattention, apathy, indecisiveness, or blocking.

7. Loss of interest in previously pleasurable activities, including sex and work.

8. Self-reproach or guilt of unrealistic proportion in an obsessional manner.

9. Thoughts of death or suicide.

Older depressives report more physical symptoms and complaints, express less guilt, and report feeling "depressed" to a lesser degree than in the younger age groups. Paranoid symptoms ranging from suspiciousness to frank delusions are commoner in the elderly, and at the place of work may be directed at peers or supervisors.

MASKED DEPRESSION

This syndrome, also known as the depressive equivalent, can involve one-third or more of patients with depression, and is believed to be more common in the elderly.[6] Usually the patients present a multitude of somatic complaints that do not respond to symptomatic treatment. These are the patients who "shop around" from doctor to doctor. Some of them may eventually undergo unnecessary surgery. The high frequency of physical illness among the elderly makes the diagnosis of masked depression difficult and challenging.

It is interesting that masked depression is more common with increasing age. Probably the aging individual becomes more aware of the interior of the body. The decline of genital libido is accompanied by a shift of residual libido to the alimentary tract so that functions such as eating and defecation become hypercathected. It is easy to understand that hypochondriasis may develop as an intrinsic part of a depressive illness. Such patients may complain of pain in any part of the body—the head, neck, and back are common sites, as well as the abdomen. They may have tried self-medication before seeking medical advice. Although appearing depressed, they may stoutly deny this; but inquiry may reveal other signs of depression, such as weight loss, anorexia, anhedonia, and decline in interest and activity in sex and work.

Any aging employee in whom depression is suspected should be questioned closely about suicidal ideation. Depressed subjects with hypochondriasis are at somewhat greater risk for suicide.

PSYCHOPATHOLOGY OF DEPRESSION

The psychopathology of depression in later life may be summed up in the single word *loss*. Losses in later life may be actual, threatened, or fantasied, i.e., existing only in the patient's mind.

What are the losses especially relevant to the situation of the aging employee? They are threefold: firstly, loss perceived as a decline in physical stamina, in vigor, in mental energies and capacities such as alertness, memory, and powers of concentration. Intellectual workers in particular are very sensitive to loss of creativity. Secondly, there are sensory losses of visual acuity and hearing. Loss of hearing, so common with aging, results in an increase in paranoid feelings in those predisposed,[7] and also contributes to social isolation, further increasing depressive feelings. Thirdly, there are the losses associated with impending retirement. These include loss of income in the face of persisting inflation, loss of location sometimes preceded by the "empty nest syndrome," and the anticipation of loss of status. The executive surrenders his prestigious office for the anonymity of being just one more retired person heading for the Sunbelt.

It should be noted that the older employee can tolerate the loss of love objects better than a decline in physical or mental health. Indeed, it is recognized that where poor health dictated retirement, some retirees may go on to develop severe depressions within a few months of stopping work.

Losses of the kind described above represent blows to the aging employee's narcissistic needs. There is some evidence that certain premorbid personality features are associated with depression. Those with rigid personalities and compulsiveness appear likelier to become depressed. Individuals whose self-concept depends on qualities which diminish with age, e.g., physical appearance, social power or standing, and idealization of the future, may be especially vulnerable to depression.

THE RELATIONSHIP OF DEPRESSION TO OTHER ILLNESSES

Sometimes depression may precede or accompany another underlying somatic disease in an aging employee. These may be endocrine, neurologic, neoplastic, or iatrogenic:

> Endocrine. Thyroid dysfunction may coexist with depression. In particular, myxedema may closely mimic depression, and confuse the diagnosis. Hyper-

calcemia from any cause may give rise to a mental state indistinguishable from depression.

Neurologic. Depression may follow head injury, and this should always be borne in mind as the elderly are more susceptible to falls. Early cases of Parkinson's disease may also superficially resemble depression because of the altered posture, masklike faces, and bradyphrenia. Pernicious anemia and folate deficiency are associated with depression in an unknown number of cases. It is also evident that depression may be an early manifestation of dementia or chronic organic brain disease.

Neoplasms. Pancreatic carcinoma, pulmonary neoplasms, and cerebral tumors can all begin insidiously with depression as an early sign.

Iatrogenic. Major tranquilizers can result in a syndrome of apathy, sluggishness, and poor concentration mimicking depression. Antihypertensives such as reserpine can result in severe depression presumably through depletion of catecholamine and serotonin from presynaptic neurones in the brain.

Differentiating Depression from Dementia

In both depression and dementia, cognition and memory are impaired, and apathy, inability to care for the self, delusions, agitation, and insomnia may be present. There are some differentiating points which may be helpful.[8]

1. In the history, the depressed patient does not usually show evidences of memory loss or disorientation, nor is there habit deterioration.

2. In the mental state examination, the depressed patient *does* remain oriented, if one can only make contact with him, in contrast to the patient with chronic organic brain syndrome.

3. The mood disturbance in the depressed patient is primary, and is often accompanied by irritability and hostility. The depressed patient rejects questions, in contrast to the organic patient who makes some attempt to reply, even though his responses may be irrelevant, nonsensical, or confabulatory.

4. The depressed patient ordinarily does not show signs of clear neurologic deficit, nor abnormal primitive reflexes, as may the patient with a chronic organic brain syndrome.

5. In general, the depressed patient tends to have a better integrated EEG, with preservation of basic rhythms.

6. The depressed patient may respond to a therapeutic trial of antidepressant medication. The patient with chronic organic brain syndrome is likely to react with an increase of confusion due to the central anticholingeric effect of the medication.

PARANOID STATES

With aging, the incidence of paranoid reactions increases. This is because the factors contributing to their development tend to mount with age. Thus, social isolation, general insecurity, solitary living, and, as mentioned previously, sensory defects, especially hearing loss, all increase with the passage of years. Furthermore, projective defense mechanisms are favored. These mechanisms, which are relatively primitive, lend themselves to situations in which the aging subject feels weak, threatened, or may perceive the external world imperfectly. Paranoid ideas in the case of the aging employee center upon peers or supervisors. He imagines they talk about him, malign his character, or spy upon him. Ideas of jealousy may surface, with people at work being envious of some special talent the paranoid subject believes he possesses. Such compensatory grandiosity offers amends for feelings of failure, or of inability to cope with whatever situation is threatening at work. It should also be noted that paranoid symptoms in the aging may be associated with alcohol abuse—alcoholic paranoia being well recognized as a consequence of long-continued alcoholism.

The recognition of a paranoid state in an aging employee is merely a preliminary to diagnosis, just as it would be in the case of confusion or stupor. There are three possibilities:

1. Persistent persecutory states (paraphrenia). The main features are paranoid delusions and hallucinations in all sensory modalities, particularly auditory, in a setting of clear consciousness. Thought disorder with flattening or incongruity of affect is rare.

2. Transitory paranoid states which include alcoholic paranoia, drug intoxications, or organic brain disease. The transitory paranoid states vary from time to time: their structure is unsystematized.

3. Paranoid personality reactions. These are morbid, but not psychotic. There are often psychopathic traits. Perhaps we should use the term "overvalued or dominant idea," instead of delusion. Many of these patients evolve into elderly eccentrics.

CHRONIC ORGANIC BRAIN SYNDROMES

Roth's forthright statement has provided the setting for consideration of chronic organic brain syndromes in aging employees:[9]

> In earlier life, organic psychoses are comparatively rare; in old age they are commonplace, and their manifestations so protean that they can never be omitted from consideration when arriving at a diagnosis. Moreover, if organic disorders are common, organic damage of a less obvious and more limited kind is ubiquitous in advanced age...the cerebrum can, therefore, never be omitted from consideration.

The commonest mode of presentation of a chronic organic brain syndrome is an employee's showing a gradual but unmistakable decline in job performance, poor judgment, and evidence of memory impairment. Assignments are forgotten, or not begun. If they are begun, they are not completed, or are marred. Materials are mislaid, and there is an obvious failure to grasp new instructions. Mood may be depressed, apathetic, or blunted. The employee may show loss of social tact, and make digestive sounds indifferent to the effect upon workmates or strangers. He neglects his appearance and grooming, and may come to work unshaven and dishevelled. Sometimes it is difficult to put a finger on a cognitive defect, but clear to recognize that there has been deterioration in personality over weeks or months.

Establishing the diagnosis of chronic organic brain syndrome depends upon a history of cognitive, memory, and affective decline, together with a definite deterioration in social behavior. The mental status examination will demonstrate memory impairment worse for recent than for remote events; some degree of disorientation; difficulties with arithmetic, with abstract thinking as, for example, in giving the meanings of proverbs; and in reasoning. There may be a change in mood, often in the direction of apathy and indifference. Behavior may become withdrawn, perhaps complicated by confusional episodes resulting in wandering away. Occasionally there may be some gross breach of social convention such as self-exposure or petty larceny. Neurologic examination often does not reveal any defect, but primitive reflexes such as the palmomental, grasp, and snout reflexes may be elicited, together with a defect of upward conjugate deviation of the eyes. Occasionally synkinesia can be demonstrated.[10] The CAT scan may demonstrate diffuse cortical atrophy and the EEG shows nonspecific diffuse dysrhythmia. Other hematologic and biochemical studies are often within normal limits.

The majority of cases are diagnosed as senile dementia of the Alzheimer type. It will be recalled that Alzheimer diagnosed his original case in a woman of 51 who had slowly become demented over a period of five years. Three stages in the clinical features of the disease have been described:[11]

> Stage I is characterized by amnesia, disturbances of spatial orientation, and lack of spontaneity. This last for 2 to 4 years, then merges into the second stage.

> Stage II is characterized by a progressive dementia involving many aspects of higher mental function, but is accompanied by focal features.

> Stage III is the final stage, where the patient is completely demented.

It should be stressed that, first, senile dementia of the Alzheimer type is by far the commonest cause of progressive mental deterioration in aging employees. Fortunately, it is not too common, but we may expect a rising prevalence over the next few years, because of the aging of the population; and, second, it is to be distinguished from normal aging, in which such features as mild, nonprogressive memory impairment, slowness, and caution are to be expected.

The diagnosis of dementia is a clinical responsibility, but such ancillary aids as the CAT scan and the EEG may be helpful. Psychological testing can also be useful. The Bender Visual Motor Gestalt Test, the Wechsler Adult Intelligence Scale, and Memory Scale may all be utilized. Wells[12] has recently reviewed the entire subject of chronic brain disease.

Because the condition is progressive, and, in our present state of knowledge, no effective treatment is known, it is important to reach a diagnosis so that afflicted employees can be reassigned to tasks within their capacity in order to keep them occupied as long as possible. Placement is a difficult problem in the face of a progressive and relentless mental handicap. It is essential to arrange for some counseling for the employee's family so that they can be informed about the course and prognosis of the condition.

Probably no more than 25 percent of chronic organic brain syndromes in the elderly are due to cerebrovascular disease, or to a variety of potentially remediable conditions such as hypothyroidism, normal pressure hydrocephalus, cerebral neoplasms, and neurosyphilis. It is axiomatic that every aging employee suspected of having a chronic organic brain syndrome is owed a full work-up to establish an accurate diagnosis. It is a failure of responsibility to apply the label "senility" and take no further action.

CONCLUSIONS

With the raising of the mandatory retirement age from 65 to 70 in the last Congress, it seems reasonable to expect an increasing number of employees working up to, and in some cases beyond, the age of 70. Inevitably, such aging employees will become more vulnerable to both functional and organic mental disorders occurring at this stage of the life cycle. In the case of such employees whose work performance is deteriorating, the geriatric psychiatrist can offer an important consultative role in establishing the diagnosis.

While the overriding consideration must always be the well-being of the individual patient, employers themselves have a vital interest in preserving a valued aging employee, who may be only temporarily handicapped by a psychiatric problem. The geriatric psychiatrists should therefore be viewed as an integral member of the health care team serving the aging employee.

DISCUSSION

Dr. Fred Charatan chaired this panel which included: Leon D. Hankoff, M.D., Professor of Psychiatry, Department of Psychiatry and Behavioral Science, Medical School, Health Sciences Center, State University of New York at Stony Brook; Stuart L. Keill, M.D., Clinical Professor and Vice Chairman of the Department of Psychiatry, State University of New York at Buffalo; Sivachandra M. Vallury, M.D., Senior Psychiatrist, South Oaks Hospital, and Assistant Professor of Clinical Psychiatry, Department of Psychiatry and Behavioral Science, Medical School, Health Sciences Center, State University of New York at Stony Brook; and Richard M. Zoppa, M.D., Senior Psychiatrist, Department of Psychiatry and Behavioral Science, Medical School, Health Sciences Center, State University of New York at Stony Brook.

Dr. Hankoff:

At Stony Brook University Hospital, in our recently opened psychiatric service, one of our first experiences with the day hospital unit has been a very impressive response on the part of the geriatric patients to this form of care. Now this is by no means a discovery, or if it is, it is certainly one of those wheels that gets discovered in psychiatry every few years—that the geriatric patient is often admirably suited to a psychiatric day hospital program. However, day hospital programs face great difficulty in obtaining funding and getting off the ground. And very few are particularly geared to the geriatric patient.

The psychiatric day hospital has three functions for the geriatric population. Firstly, the day hospital can function as an alternative to 24-hour full hospitalization, when there is a fairly acute geriatric problem. The saving achieved is striking. A patient receives a day of intensive treatment at perhaps one-third the cost of a full 24 hours of psychiatric hospitalization. A second function is to shorten the stay in the psychiatric hospital. The patient who has been admitted to an institution such as South Oaks, for instance, can be discharged to a day hospital program while still in a resolving phase of his or her disorder. Again there can be major economic savings. Third, the day hospital provides a program that allows the patient to keep both feet in the community, while receiving intensive resocialization. This might be called tertiary prevention in psychiatry. The advantages thus are lowered cost, and the maintenance of the individual in the community.

Two major problems arise in the implementation of a geriatric day hospital program. (I suppose a third should be mentioned, which is funding—that is first, last, and constant.). The first basic difficulty in developing a day hospital program is transportation. This service has to be built in, with some form of subsidized transportation, such as mini-buses, to take the patients to and from the hospital every day. Without this it is almost impossible to run a geriatric program. Second, patient recruiting is a key issue. Neither professionals nor laypeople tend to think in terms of this kind of a program. We know that it works very well, but it is not in the ordinary habit pattern to consider a day hospital as an alternative to hospitalization, or as a means of helping an individual to a higher level of functioning. Consequently a sustained effort at patient recruiting is essential if a day hospital is to work.

Dr. Zoppa:

The possible obliteration of a retirement age will probably mean more and more older employees. It therefore behooves industry and the medical profession to be in a position to identify certain psychiatric problems that will arise for these older employees. Dr. Charatan very clearly and comprehensively presented the list of not only the more common, but also the less common problems which may beset the aging employee. Some thoughts might be added on one of these—depression—perhaps the most common reversible illness of this group. Dr. Charatan pointed out that loss is a primary dynamic feature in depression, and it has been my experience that one aspect of loss, which is change, has not been paid enough attention with regard to employees. Of course we know that most individuals, whether young or old, would react unfavorably if their job was taken away, or their house burned down, or if someone dear to them died. This is no great discovery. However, many employees on reaching a certain age, get kicked upstairs, so to speak. They get promoted to a job which is presumably an easy berth, and the employee himself may be anxiously anticipating this. The individual now has a "better job," but a month or two later, for reasons unaccountable to the family, or to the employer, the individual begins to feel depressed. He does not perform as well, functioning becomes impaired in many areas, and eventually he sees a psychiatrist. I think that it behooves industry to be aware that the older individual is sensitive to change. Furthermore, if you have a person who is suffering from what might be either dementia or depression, it makes sense to treat that person with the appropriate modality rather than to chalk it up to old age, and leave the individual alone to continue to deteriorate.

Dr. Keill:

A couple of points I would like to make might be symbolized by a clinical experience early in my career. I was a young, inexperienced psychiatrist who, as part of my training, had been assigned to a neurological unit on the west side of Manhattan, and I was appropriately humble and obsequious when the neurology resident made his rounds. I was on duty one night when a woman was brought in in a coma with a number of very serious neurological signs. The neurology resident came through, and after a cursory look at my notes and the patient, and a couple of taps in appropriate places on the woman's body, said, "Well, she won't last the night. She has a rapidly growing tumor, which is on the left side of the base of the brain. Give her some fluids. Don't bother me if she doesn't survive for the morning rounds, but get permission for an autopsy."

I gave her fluids and sat with her, a bit puzzled, dozing off from time to time. Curiously, by the time morning came around she was almost imperceptibly better. We hadn't done anything for her except keep her quiet and give her fluids. Over the next couple of days she slowly began to improve, and we discovered, after some more complex diagnostic procedures, that she was suffering from a rare condition known as bromism.

This was a patient whose history was fairly replete with the kind of factors that Dr. Charatan touched on so pointedly. A year or so before admission, she had been discharged from her job because of cutbacks, and she was one of the older people in the organization. Even though she was one of the more effective employees, she had been terminated from a work that she had performed in various capacities for almost 30 years. At about the same period a major disruption took place in her family. A daughter married, started a family, and moved away. In subtle and in not-so-subtle ways, the woman got the message that she was a nuisance, that her children knew how to raise their children, and didn't even need her to babysit, much less give advice. She became depressed and preoccupied with this situation, and began to experience minor somatic difficulties. She went to a number of physicians who, I regret to say, responded to the complaints with "Well, when you get to be old, what can you expect?" Finally, having gotten the brush-off from her employer, her family, and a number of physicians, she found something called Bromo Seltzer, which seemed to make her feel better. She took it once a day, and then she discovered that when she took it twice a day, she felt even better: not euphoric, but just less troubled and less aware of physical discomforts. Gradually the Bromo Seltzer began to build up in her system, and she developed an acute case of bromism.

Happily, when we discovered what was what, we worked out, with the help of a very capable social service department, a whole new life for her—not a new career, but a new life, with some surrogate children, as well as activities in volunteer groups, and she did very well.

I believe there is a lesson in this, because one of the things that I have seen from three perspectives—as head of an acute hospital treatment unit, as an employer of a number of people of different age groups and different talents, and as a physician in the private practice of psychotherapy—that one can begin to detect the anlage, if you will, of this kind of a story early on. With the proper sensitivity to the realities of the system, to the patient and to the family, one can sometimes prevent what literally was in this case, (and in hundreds and hundreds of others), life-threatening situations.

Dr. Charatan referred to the empty-nest syndrome, which we often connect with the middle-aged individual, whose children have grown up and gone. There is a variation of the empty-nest syndrome—the empty-nest-for-the-grandparent syndrome, in which their own children, who may have stayed in the neighborhood, are saying, ''We don't need you, and we are only concerned that you are not going to end up in a nursing home because we wouldn't want *that*, but *we* can't take care of you.''

This is a very frightening double message. It is a double message delivered in terms of love, but it is a clear rejection. Even for the basically well-adjusted older individual it is hard to accept this in what might be considered a ''mature'' way, and say, ''I understand, and I won't complain, and I won't feel badly about it, and I'll move on.'' I think that we, as health and social service providers, must take much of the responsibility for the development of this system.

Dr. Vallury:

Bernice Neugarten, who has done a great deal of work on aging, wrote a beautiful article in 1979, *Time, Age, and Life Cycle.* The history she presents is that between 1940 and 1950 much study was done regarding older people, who were looked on as desolate and destitute and who fell under the aegis of physicians and social workers. Also, at this time, child psychiatry inaugurated longitudinal studies. When gerontology and pediatrics met in the middle, so to speak, the middle-age crisis came into play. This was further reinforced by media hype.

All of us are brought up to be legends unto ourselves. People in the United States dream of becoming president. A legend starts with implied wish fulfillment. The problem comes as time starts running out, and wishes remain just wishes. All of us have a mental clock built into us. We go to school, we get married, we have children, and become grandparents. It is not aging that is the crisis situation. All of us, especially with older parents, anticipate death and dying.

The point I would like to make is that aging is not a disease. It is a part of a biological process, and with it brings all the strengths that we have accumulated through experience and maturation. The entire process can be divided into three phases: the young adult who tries to get ahead, but at the same time wants to plant his roots; middle age, where relationships are looked at anew; and old age, with a gradual decathecting from the world outside. If you speak to anyone in the old-age group, it is not that they fear death; it is mainly dependency and deterioration that they fear. The issue is that if one is granted security in society, then old age becomes a little more palatable.

Audience:

I think one of the real dilemmas facing employers, both public and private, is that the people who are likely to stay until they are age 70 or older are those who have no other options—those who have not developed a sense of involvement in other activities, people who may be under the gun financially. In other words, organizations may be stuck with people they don't want. Whereas the real go-getters, people with a great sense of self-worth, a sense of purpose, a sense of planning for the future, are the ones who are likely not to stay. They are likely to leave and move on to new challenges which they are able to develop for themselves. Is this not then a setting in which psychiatric and psychological problems are apt to become much more severe than if there were options available for everybody?

Dr. Keill:

It has been said, In his talk, Dan Knowles said, and I fully agree, that one should not make a rule that everybody must retire at any age, because in that way you are going to eliminate some of the good with the bad. However, I believe that there are not always enough administrative people around who can make the choice and say, we'll keep this one because he is good, and we'll encourage this one to retire because he is not good. In a number of areas, particularly in larger governmental organizations, this is really not what happens. People who last the longest are often the ones who cause the least trouble and who have the least creativity.

I would love to see a situation occur in which people could be kept on until age 95 if they were interested and able to perform. But in order to make that work, and to combat discrimination because of chronological age, one has to bite the bullet and also say that if people who at 55, or 35, or 24, can't do the work they should be encouraged then to start their second career.

Dr. Charatan:

There is an undoubted difference between psychological and chronological age. Age is partly objective, according to years, and it is also partly subjective. It is worth a reminder that the age of 65 was set as the appropriate age for retirement in the time of Bismarck, when social legislation was enacted in Germany. It is also important to recognize that our own society has a considerable fear, almost a phobia, of aging and death. This point is very fully discussed in Christopher Lasch's book, *The Culture of Narcissism,* which I strongly recommend to you for one chapter alone, on aging and death. Lasch suggests that pre-retirement counseling is really, if you look at it in a negative way, a form of self-destruct for certain older workers who are approaching the point at which their organization would like them to retire. This brings us back to this question that those who hold onto their jobs may do so for a number of reasons: not only that they would feel insecure with any change, but also, perhaps, for economic reasons, personal reasons. Every case therefore would have to be judged on its individual merits, rather than by our saying, arbitrarily, that somebody should be forced out of a job which they want to hold onto, and which they can reasonably perform.

Audience:

I'd like to make the observation that I think a day hospital program does not provide an effective coping system for the aged. Many times a senior citizen would like to stay in the work community, but the friction areas are usually with the family. I believe a night hospital program, where the person could go to work and then come back to a medical center for psychiatric treatment and for easement back into the community, is much more needed.

Dr. Hankoff:

You are absolutely right. If a day hospital is going to disrupt a working arrangement, then it is working against itself. It certainly is not appropriate for anyone who has roots in the daytime community in terms of any kind of gainful employment or involvement on a voluntary basis. We have been speaking of a day hospital for people who no longer have that capacity. However, one partial answer to the problem is the integration of family therapy and family techniques into any kind of a day hospital. With regard to night hospitalization for the working patient, it is a good idea and I always try it, and it almost never works. It is appropriate for just an incidental segment of the patient population.

Audience:

I think the retired people can be re-utilized in a number of ways—they could be used to help train younger employees, or they could get active in the Gray Panthers, or go back to school.

Dr. Charatan:

I think the issue you are raising is how should people retire. Should they retire partially, to start with, rather than completely, or should they retire from one career to, say, another career, or should they even retire to avocations.

Elliot Slater, a famous British psychiatrist, said many years ago that every one of us will go to the grave with only a fraction of our potential realized. I don't know if that statement is a psychiatric one or a religious one; it may be a little of both. It is certainly important to consider the fate of the older retired employee from your point of view, which is what they should do after they retire, whether fully or partially.

Audience:

What I have heard so far is the discussion of the treatment of sick people. I would like to refocus our attention on the employee, the person who is working and is getting older. Can this individual produce for the dollar he is earning or should he be replaced by someone younger? What can industry do to retain the individual who is getting older in his job and offer his expertise, his knowledge, to the younger person coming up who, in turn, is getting older, so that we don't increase our patient loads in hospitals, day centers, or night centers. I would recommend to those of you who are representatives of industry to tell your medical departments that, perhaps in addition to the internist, the cardiologist, and the surgeon, you have a consultant liaison psychiatrist on the staff. This psychiatrist is available to see the individual employee who is beginning to show signs of aging that are interfering with his productivity or his relationship with his fellow workers so that something can be done to abort, if possible, the ravages of the oncoming aging process.

Dr. Charatan:

You have put your finger on a most important aspect of our discussion and that is, the prevention of breakdown in the older employee who presumably is of considerable value to his organization.

Dr. Zoppa:

The problem becomes very complex. It is not a simple matter of what do we do individually, or even as a small group, which can change concepts that have taken many years to develop. What you are really asking is, what is the history of the aging, the elderly, in a community? I think that in former generations, older individuals in many of the Western societies, as in many primitive societies today, were very much a part of the entire community, and their thoughts and opinions were sought and listened to. The concept that the older individual is not a worthwhile person, is someone to be shunned, to be cast aside, is, I think, a more recent development. The idea that man, out of his own good will, will change, is perhaps a naive one. Government will have to be the instrument, as far as I can see, to enact certain laws that will begin to allow people then to examine themselves, to examine their aging employee, to examine aging *individuals*, because, really, the issue extends beyond the worker.

Dr. Hankoff:

I think, in a sense, we are all on the same side. However, I do think that it is confusing the issue when we talk about the detection and the early treatment of what will clearly become a psychiatric disorder, with symptoms and dysfunction; and confuse that with habits of living, the ability to renew one's self, to develop a second career, all of the broader factors which are built into our culture and society.

Dr. Keill:

I think that the concept of primary prevention to provide an atmosphere in which mental illness will be less likely to develop is a valid notion. It is sometimes hard to document, however, and it certainly takes a long time. I think the concept of secondary prevention is where we should focus. Secondary prevention includes, for example, the early detection of some malfunction of the individual, the evaluation of the physical status of that individual. Is the malfunction really an early symptom of some organic damage? Is it because the patient is abusing some substance? Or, is it a reflection of the social milieu, either the patient's family setting or the work setting, or both? With this social and clinical evaluation, one can often eliminate some of the causes and restore the individual to full functioning.

Dr. Charatan:

Yes, I could encapsulate it by saying that the way a corporation should approach deteriorating performance, let's say in an older employee, would be to have the supervisor call him on the carpet and say, "Gridley, your output of widgits is falling," or "You are less creative," or "Your sales curve is taking a nose dive." Then I think it would be up to the supervisor to determine whether Gridley's failure is due to loss of interest in his job, or whether, in fact, it is the beginning of some kind of psychiatric disorder, rather than simply dismissing it by saying, well, Gridley's getting too old, he'll have to go. I think that is the really crucial issue.

Audience:

The cliche is that as we age a few of us may mellow like fine wine, but most of us grow rigid and inflexible. Do you see this as a myth or as a real problem?

Dr. Vallury:

I think it is a myth. Each person is very complex. There is no uniform course and no format regarding aging in general. Up to a point there is a commonality, but as one grows older and as the path lengthens, each life becomes more highly individual. One pitfall not to fall into is generalizing on problems in trying to find an easy solution.

Dr. Zoppa:

Whether or not some people will grow old like a fine wine or turn to vinegar depends, I think, on the individual's premorbid personality. Some people tend to age very well. Those are the individuals who throughout life have faced adversities and challenges with a certain degree of flexibility. They simply have the ego strengths, if you will, to go on and accept whatever is coming along in life at whatever age.

Audience:

One thing I have observed with employees who are eligible to retire, who are collecting Social Security or a pension, is that their attitudes and work ethics seem to change. They no longer feel that they *have* to work, so they have a different attitude. They are working because they want to work, and that imparts a tremendous psychological lift. I don't know of any organizations that say to an employee, when you reach this particular point, when you don't need to work any more, you come back to us and we'll let you pick a job that is open, with some kind of salary adjustment. The industrial world has no capacity for allowing a career change within the same organization. They push you out the door, and then you have to find that second career in the outside world.

Dr. Charatan:

Yes, once again you are pointing to the all-or-nothing law of corporations—either you do this job, or you retire, and there is no place for you on either a part-time basis or in any other capacity. However, there may well be a changing attitude on the part of corporations, because with the increasing number of older people and with the need for the older employee to maintain his integrity as well as his independence, perhaps the time is coming when we may see more of what you are suggesting.

I would like to return for a moment to the question whether people become more mellow like fine wine, or whether they become more rigid, and perhaps even paranoid. I think it was Simone De Beauvoir who wrote in *The Coming of Age*, people age as they have lived. There is great truth in that, because premorbid personality certainly does play an important role in aging. We can think, of course, of many people who continue to be extremely creative and productive into very ripe old age. Michelangelo was one. Grandma Moses painted her most famous picture, *Christmas Eve*, at the age of 100 and died the next year.

It is clear to me, as a geriatric psychiatrist, that a great deal more research needs to be done in this area. However, I do know three simple pieces of advice to give to those approaching retirement. One, stay involved. Two, stay in training—a prudent diet and daily, lifelong exercise are important ingredients of that recipe. And three, and I think perhaps most important, is stay in love.

Audience:

Indirectly I have heard two things that I would like to clarify: if you are young, you are not qualified, if you are old, you are qualified. I think it depends on the individual. There are very young people who are highly qualified and very old people who are totally unqualified. I haven't heard anyone addressing continuing education in the job you are holding. I think the health field is an excellent example of having had mandatory continuing education because we all found it very comfortable to sit back in the old slots and carry on.

Dr. Keill:

As a matter of fact, when Dr. Charatan mentioned the second rule of keeping in training, I thought he was talking about continuing education in the job. We in the health professions have had to have this imposed on us from the outside. I think that it is terribly important. As long as you can keep training an individual, and as long as you can make the individual keep recognizing for himself the importance of learning something, you are going to avoid an awful lot of depression and deterioration. This is one of the principles that I use with my own patients. They have to keep expanding their horizons in whatever area they choose, and it may be in the area of their work, it may be in the area of their avocation, it may be in preparation for a second career, 20 years hence.

Dr. Hankoff:

Statistically, an aged population shows greater variability than a young population. If you look at 1,000 17-year-olds, for instance, they have a sharp bell-shaped curve. If you look at 1,000 aged people, let's say age 70 for argument's sake, you have a much wider, much flatter curve. They are much more variable, a much more different group of people. You might even say a more interesting group. Another point I'd like to raise, has any thought been given to affirmative action in terms of hiring people for given age levels? I would propose that it be considered.

Audience:

There is a responsibility of people in a supervisory capacity to have a process occur with an employee from the day when they meet one another for the first time, so that when the time comes when a person is in trouble, there is a relationship established between the employee and the employer. It makes it easy to help him deal with these problems and to set him in the right direction towards seeking help and support on the job. Then it doesn't come to him as a shock at the last minute.

Dr. Charatan:

I agree that the role of the supervisor is very important in recognizing when an older employee is having some kind of problem on the job reflected in his performance. On the other hand, I think that one must also not overlook the importance of the peer group, the fellow workers. We tend to overlook that. There is no question that an older worker also has to, in some ways, conform to the peer group, to same-aged employees working alongside him who are quite sensitive to any changes in behavior or performance that might conceivably reflect a psychiatric condition.

Audience:

When supervisors discriminate against somebody for whatever reason they should be made aware of the psychological effect of their discriminatory acts. Very often they make them strictly on the basis of a managerial decision. If the budget is going to be cut and they have to get rid of some positions, they get rid of the highest-salaried people and fill in with lower-grade employees. They don't really see what is happening to the individual; they are not made to look at the person they are discriminating against. I know of a case where a supervisor discriminated against an employee on the basis of age. Now that man is undergoing psychological fracture and is filing a discrimination case. It has had a tremendous impact on him. But the supervisor is unaware. He is only aware of his own perspective as a manager.

Dr. Charatan:

Are you recommending some kind of sensitivity training for supervisors and managers in corporations?

Audience:

When a discrimination case is filed, the supervisor should have some kind of a screening board that he is brought to, to see if in fact the decision he made was discriminatory. Maybe then he would at least be able to rectify at that level, or at a future time reconsider the employee in some other respect.

Dr. Keill:

I am not sure that I, for one, understand how you would teach that person that he was discriminating. We all know that discrimination goes on all the time, yet I wonder how many of you, sophisticated human services people, could stop and think of a time when you have been discriminatory against someone else. It is very hard because you rationalize beautifully. We all do. You say, no, it really wasn't because she was old, it was because she didn't understand the new technical aspects of the job or she is too rigid, or, I didn't really bump this person because he was old, it was just because he doesn't get along with anybody else in the office and therefore I had to do it. It is very hard to look at ourselves honestly and say, yes, that was a discriminatory thing; that was a bad management practice, and it was also an inhuman thing to do. I am not sure, even if we got people involved forcibly in sensitivity training whether we would be able to encourage people to be that open with themselves.

Audience:

Are there more major psychiatric implications to letting older people go prematurely from work situations than from keeping younger people away from opportunities to come into systems? I realize this is a very general, broad question but I am wondering if there is some general answer.

Dr. Charatan:

I think it is rather clear that there will always be a continuing conflict between older employees whose time for retirement is approaching, and the entry of new, younger employees on the bottom rungs of the ladder in any organization. I think that is clearly the dilemma of our time.

I can think of a personal example here of an older physician who was planning to retire from quite an important position in medicine, and after he had gone through all the preparations for retirement, he had to change his mind because he felt that he simply could not retire on what he had managed to save. That is obviously an extreme example, but I think it points up the problem. I think that where older employees have made some adequate provisions for their retirement, where they have thought this through and perhaps have had some pre-retirement counseling, which incidentally is always said to be most effective within three to five years of retirement, then I think they will be more ready to retire. They will have mapped out their life ahead of the time when they are going to relinquish their major paid occupation for whatever they are going to relinquish it for. It seems to me again that retirement has to be a planned and well-considered change in life style.

Dr. Vallury:

Retirement usually is anticipated by most people, at some depth, at some level. Now if I was a workaholic who avoided family contact by putting in 18 hours, I am going to have a very rough time when the axe falls on me. But if I had other avocations and work was not the all-important thing that gave me an identity, I would be much more able to adjust to what is going to happen.

Dr. Keill:

As Dr. Charatan said, the old *must* always give way to the young, but who is going to decide when? Pre-retirement counseling is valid in theory, but the question is, who is going to make the decision when *I* am going to go for pre-retirement counseling? Are they going to say, you 15 people, according to our personnel records, are due, or do I say, I am going to be retiring in a few years and I think it might be worthwhile. I feel that while I may be ready to make the decision, I don't want to have anybody else telling me they are making the decision for me, that I am now old enough to move on.

Dr. Vallury:

I would like to share a slight paradox. We have never had a president under 35 nor many senators under that either, yet it is the biggest corporation in a sense. There are different rules for the same game and we are all trying to equalize it and put some logic into the situation.

Dr. Zoppa:

In answer to the question as to whether it would be psychiatrically more detrimental for the individual to push out an older person or to keep a younger person waiting, I think it would be more difficult for the older person to have to put up with the gold watch and the pat on the back. The younger person has more resources available. If he doesn't get job A he can always try and get job B, whereas the man who is 60 or 65 and ready to be pushed out is not likely to find anything. That would certainly be a precipitant for alcoholism, along with depression, and a variety of other problems.

Audience:

I wonder how many workers really look forward to retirement and don't want to work any longer. I wonder what the percentage is of people who want to continue and others who are happy to retire.

Dr. Charatan:

Although we have tended to see retirement as something that is forced on the individual, I think it is also important to be aware that many people do look forward to retirement. There are many people who do not have a vast reservoir of stamina, who may not be in the best of health, and who look forward to retirement as a release from humdrum work and drudgery. So that retirement can be looked upon in all kinds of ways. I think we shouldn't fall into the trap of thinking that retirement is something that is always forced upon us. Obviously, as Dr. Keill implied, it is best if retirement can be a voluntary thing. The individual realizes that it is time for him to separate from his work and whether he wants to move into a serial career or go into volunteer work, take up some kind of avocation, is entirely a matter for him to decide. I think the point that we are all making is that this should be decided within 3 to 5 years of the time when the person is planning to leave his work. You will find an excellent review of retirement in the book by Bromley, entitled *The Psychology of Human Aging.* It is very comprehensive and it gives you an excellent analysis of attitudes towards retirement.

REFERENCES

1. Palmore, E., & Maddox, G.L. *Sociological Aspects of Aging, in Behavior and Adaptation in Late Life.* E. W. Busse and E. Pfeiffer, eds. Boston: Little Brown & Co., 1977, 42.

2. Bromley, D.B. *The Psychology of Human Aging* (2nd ed.). Harmondsworth, Middlesex, England: Penguin Books, 1974, 254.

3. Zimberg, S. Two Types of Problem Drinkers: Both Can Be Managed. *Geriatrics,* 1974, *29,* 135.

4. Schuckit, M.A., & Pastor, P.A. Jr. *Alcohol related Psychopathology in the Aged, in Psychopathology of Aging.* Kaplan O.J., Ed. New York: Academic Press, 1979, 211.

5. American Psychiatric Association. Diagnostic and Statistical Manual of Mental Disorders (3rd ed.). Washington D.C., 1980.

6. Lesse, S. *Masked Depression.* New York: Jason Aronson, 1974.

7. Cooper, A.F. Deafness and Paranoid Illness. *British Journal of Psychiatry,* 1976, *129,* 216.

8. Charatan, F.B. Psychiatric Syndromes in the Aged. *Hillside J. Clin. Psychiatry* 1. 143, 1979.

9. Roth, M. Classification and Aetiology in Mental Disorders of Old Age. In D.W.K. Kay and A. Walk (Eds.), *Recent Developments in Psychogeriatrics,* Ashford, Kent, England. Headley Bros., 1971, 1.

10. Adams, G.F. *Cerebrovascular Disability and the Aging Brain.* Edinburgh and London: Churchill Livingston, 1974, 47.

11. Pearce, J., & Miller, E. *Clinical Aspects of Dementia.* London: Bailliere Tindall, 1973, 23.

12. Wells, C.E. Chronic Brain Disease: An Overview. *American Journal of Psychiatry,* 1978, *135,* 1.

Chapter 2

MIDDLE-AGED AND OLDER WORKERS: AN INDUSTRY PERSPECTIVE

*Daniel E. Knowles**

When I got to be 39 years of age, I suddenly woke up and saw myself becoming 40 and I couldn't believe it. I knew that the Age Discrimination Act protected people starting at age 40, and I decided that, at last, I was going to get to belong to one of the protected classes. All of us, God willing, get to belong to that group of middle-aged and older workers. When I was 39 I was invited by the National Council on Aging to attend a seminar on the subject in Carmel, California. That was really the first awakening. I figured anyone who would pay my way and put me up at a fancy resort deserved to get something back, so I ended up getting on an industry advisory committee with the National Council on Aging, and that started me off.

*Mr. Knowles is Director of Personnel for the Grumman Aerospace Corporation, a firm with more than 21,000 employees. He majored in Psychology and received his Master's degree from Hofstra University.

Mr. Knowles was formerly President of the Long Island Personnel Directors Association, and is also on the faculty of the New York Institute of Technology where he teaches courses on personnel management, collective bargaining, and labor relations. He has also lectured for the American Management Association and the National Metal Trades Association. He is writing a book pertaining to industry affirmative action for the middle-aged and older worker.

Since that time I have had opportunities to testify in Congress, about three times to the House and once to the Senate.

I might add that we are fortunate that out of three of the leading proponents in Congress of the middle-aged and older worker, New York State happens to be blessed with two, Senator Jacob Javits, and also one of our own locals, The Honorable Thomas Downey, whom I have found to be exceptionally supportive.

One of the things that has made my talk easier was that several months ago I got a phone call from Washington asking me if I would prepare a paper on middle-aged and older workers for President Carter's Special Committee on Aging. So, for the formal part of my paper, I would like to share with you the thoughts that I submitted to President Carter's Committee.

Before giving an industry perspective on this subject, I would first like to set the scene. In the past, both Federal and state legislation has sought to protect individuals against unfair treatment in employment by passing relatively unenforceable laws prohibiting discrimination on the basis of race, religion, age, sex, national origin, and so on. When President Kennedy came into office, a new dimension was added through a concept of affirmative action—a concept that went beyond the negativism of antidiscrimination legislation. With Executive Order 11246 we witnessed the beginning of a positive approach to the problems of discrimination. Initially the thrust of affirmative action was directed towards minorities, which included Blacks, Orientals, Native Americans, and Hispanics.

Despite contrary opinions from minorities and government, industry will be quick to convince any objective person of the tremendous strides minorities have made in their representation in the broad EEO-1 job categories of officials and managers, professionals, sales, technicians, office and clerical, skilled crafts persons, semiskilled operatives, and the unskilled laborers and service workers. Today many companies can claim that at least in these broad categories, minorities are well represented in relation to their availability in the labor market as reported in demographics of the 1970 census figures. While the job of affirmative action has not been completed for minorities, significant progress, nevertheless, has been made in the past 15-plus years.

With the visible success of affirmative action for minorities in the 60's, this concept was extended to women in the work force through the Equal Pay Law and other legislation. During the past 10 years, considerable progress has been made in relation to women in industry. Although women have a longer way to go than the minorities, significant changes in the representation of women in professional jobs beyond the traditional professions of nursing and teaching have taken place.

The Federal government passed legislation via Section 503 of the Rehabilitation Act of 1973 to establish "affirmative action" for handicapped people. In addition, a fourth group was added to those protected via affirmative action programs—veterans, with special emphasis on the Vietnam and the handicapped veteran, under Section 402 of the Vietnam-era Veterans Readjustment Assistance Act of 1974.

Because of overlap, it is difficult to determine accurately the percentage of the total work force that falls into these four categories, but it is substantial.

A greater number of people, namely Catholics, Jews, people of Southern and Middle-European ancestry, and middle-aged and older workers (age 40 to 70) are protected via antidiscrimination legislation, but not by affirmative action legislation. Either the Federal government considers discrimination against these groups to be less severe, political pressure has not been brought to bear in their interests, or these groups are thought to be less important.

Affirmative action-oriented programs protecting minorities, women, the handicapped, and veterans provide that every employer doing business with the Federal government under a contract for more than $2,500 must take affirmative action to hire these groups. Affirmative action also applies to job assignments, promotions, training, transfers, pay, working conditions, terminations, and so on. About half of all the businesses in the United States, some 3 million, are covered by this legislation. Each government contractor holding a contract or subcontract of $50,000 or more, and having at least 50 employees, is required to develop and maintain an affirmative action program which sets forth the policies and practices regarding these groups. *This program must be reviewed and updated each year.*

In summary, affirmative action is a positive program. Basically, it is not a punitive program as yet: there are numerous avenues for recourse in the event of perceived discrimination. Each contractor, in addition, must include an affirmative action clause in each of its contracts or subcontracts. The clause must cover at least the following points: the contractor agrees not to discriminate against any of the four groups qualified to perform the job, and also agrees to take affirmative action to hire, advance, and treat these people without discrimination. The contractor agrees to abide by all Department of Labor rules and regulations. In the event of noncompliance the contractor will be declared in default. The contractor agrees to post notices of affirmative action in conspicuous places in the plant. The contractor agrees to notify all union or worker representatives that they are covered by the affirmative action law. The contractor also must include the affirmative action clause in all subcontracts on purchase orders of more than $2,500.

Typically, a company of 25,000 employees may have a plan which, including its work-force analysis, will end up as 20 volumes and perhaps 5,000 pages. It has been reported that General Electric has an entire room filled from the floor to the ceiling with affirmative action plans from its various plants in the United States.

Is it any wonder, with the full weight of the Federal government, through its various legislative annual audits by the Office of Federal Contract Compliance of the Department of Labor, the Equal Employment Opportunity Commission, and various state and county Human Rights Commissions, that the quality of life, in general, has improved for groups covered by affirmative action programs?

Affirmative action programs are big business within big business today. Millions of dollars each year are spent by government and business to ensure compliance with the law.

Any person with a sensitive conscience could not deny the importance and rightness of affirmative action for minorities, women, the handicapped, and veterans. The statistics show a substantial difference in the median income of minorities and women, as against others not included in these groups. The quarrel is not with government and its concern with these groups, but rather with the benign neglect the government has demonstrated towards the middle-aged and older workers—the forgotten Americans who represent the largest of the so-called protected groups.

In 1967, Congress passed the Age Discrimination Employment Act. Its motivation is obscure. Whether due to pressure from such organizations as the National Council on Aging, senior citizens' groups, or an awareness of protection for other groups under other laws and executive orders, it nevertheless focused attention on the question of discrimination. For some strange reason, the Wage and Hour Division of the Department of Labor was assigned the responsibility for enforcement of its antidiscrimination provisions. Unfortunately, the Wage and Hour Division was supplied few resources in terms of manpower and training of its limited personnel to provide adequate information on the subject to industry, much less police its enforcement. It was estimated by some officials of the Department of Labor that an additional 2,000 trained employees would be needed to do the job.

The message to industry 13 years following the enactment of the Act remains ambiguous. In summary, the message has been: Do not overtly discriminate against the middle-aged or older worker especially by policies that effect groups of such employees. The Age Discrimination Employment Act's impact on industry has been minimal. It is more an occasional irritant in comparison to the action-oriented positive thrust of affirmative action programs for other groups. While the effect on industry of the Age Discrimination Employment Act may be minimal, the impact on the middle-aged and older worker has been one of benign neglect. The middle-aged and older workers represent the largest of the so-called "minority groups" in the United States' work force. The most insidious type of discrimination taking place today is waged against this group for several reasons. First, much of the discrimination is subconscious and subtle. People discriminating against the older worker are not even aware that they are discriminating. Second, age discrimination is insidious because it is perpetuated by other older workers, and not by younger people who are not in the management positions to do the discriminating. It is like predator that devours its own. Third, since the middle-aged and older workers are the largest of the so-called protected groups, more cases of discrimination probably occur against them on the sheer weight of statistics.

Unfortunately, the full impact of discrimination on the older worker will never be fully understood because of the subtleties, and the poor statistical data maintained by the various state employment agencies. Statistics indicate that the older worker, once laid off, takes nearly twice as long to get back into the work force as younger people. When someone's unemployment benefits are exhausted, he or she is no longer carried as a statistic. Many older workers, once unemployed, eventually give up and become involuntarily retired.

Let's take a look at Congress. In passing the Age Discrimination Employment Act in 1967, Congress has merely addressed the tip of the iceberg. While the law offers an avenue for recourse to a person who is discriminated against, it does nothing to provide an environment within industry in which discrimination is ended. With the exception of protection in the pension and fringe benefits areas, remedial aid is provided only following acts of discrimination. Paradoxically, even when the Age Discrimination Employment Act was revised, it merely extended protection of the law, such as it is, to another couple of million people between the ages of 65 and 70. Would it not have been better to improve the quality of life in employment for the over 30 million workers between the ages of 40 and 65.

If Congress accepts the fact that the Age Discrimination Employment Act has not kept pace with other legislation in the area of discrimination, it should enact a further revision of the Act to accomplish the following as a minimum:

1. Direct the Department of Labor to do a statistical analysis within Federal, state, and local agencies in the area of discrimination by nature of complaint.

2. Direct the Department of Labor to enact education programs in industry pertaining to the nature of the middle-aged worker.

3. Direct the Department of Labor to research and disseminate to industry in sufficient quantitites information exploding the myths about the middle-aged and older worker, on the model of its publication pertaining to women.

4. Direct the Department of Labor to provide industry detailed demographic information by skills and age, the better to assess how companies measure up to the availability of older workers in the work force.

Essentially, it should, through legislation, be the goal of Congress to require the Department of Labor to institute a meaningful program of voluntary compliance to the concepts of a "fair shake" for the middle-aged and older worker. Industry cannot and will not meet the demands of these people unless Congress directs the Department of Labor to provide industry with the tools to do so. No one in industry, and not many representatives of the Wage and Hour Division of the Department of Labor, want to see a further proliferation of paperwork programs in the area of affirmative action. Congress should ensure that the Department of Labor does its share to help industry and ultimately the middle-aged and older worker. Industry, if given the tools and the opportunity to take voluntary affirmative action towards the older worker, cannot place blame for failure anywhere else. Failure to comply voluntarily to the principle of fairness to these groups of middle-aged and older workers might subsequently require further revisions of the Age Discrimination Employment Act calling for annual formal affirmative action plans similar to those of other protected groups.

Let us now look at the Department of Labor. If Congress and the Age Discrimination Employment Act constitute an expression of benign neglect towards the middle-aged and older worker, then the Department of Labor's neglect can be characterized as unresponsive and insensitive to the condition of such workers. With the exception of investigating the claims of discrimination by groups or individuals, I perceive no evidence of any affirmative or positive steps by the Department of Labor in either assisting such groups toward the goals or improving their conditions of employment.

Following testimony on several occasions to the various House and Senate Committees on aging, I finally prevailed on Representative Fred Rooney, Chairman of the Select Committee on Aging, to write to the Honorable F. Ray Marshall, Secretary of Labor. Almost 3 years later there still does not appear to be a voluntary response from the Department of Labor to any of the above recommendations to Congress. Perhaps the enactment into law of this or similar recommendations will provide the Department of Labor with the motivation to attack this insidious form of discrimination. An ad hoc committee within the Department of Labor is needed to prepare a

"How To Do It" booklet encompassing an awareness section depicting the plight of the middle-aged and older worker. Included should be sections devoted to the exploding of the myths about the older worker, such as "you can't teach an old dog new tricks," demographic information pertaining to the work force, and a format to demonstrate how a company should undertake a self-analysis of its work force by age.

Failure by the Department of Labor to take some of the positive steps suggested above will only convince American industry of the indifference and laissez-faire attitude towards this important segment of our work force.

As for industry's perception of the middle-aged and older worker: industry has at least one similarity to Congress and the Department of Labor—all three are pragmatists. Each group pays lip service to the concept of the dignity of all mankind, all Americans, and even all the heterogeneous groups that make up our work force. Yet industry in general is quick to respond to the pressures of running a business. These pressures can take the form of production, quality, schedule, costs, budgets, sales, and yes, even affirmative action programs for protected groups. Affirmative action programs have been an industry priority for the past 15 years or more. Failure to comply means sanction; consequently affirmative action programs have become "must jobs" within industry. Concern for the middle-aged and older worker, at best, is a "should" or "like to do" job and, at worst, is completely unknown to a major segment of industry today.

If the average company were asked if it discriminates against the middle-aged and older worker, I am sure it would reply indignantly that it does not. In answer, I submit that probably not one company in 10,000 has ever even researched its own organization and made comparisons with the limited work-force availability statistics provided by the Department of Labor. We are all caught up in the youth cult, and we are all its victims. What manager of a department isn't looking, when in need of additional help, for a 26-year-old college graduate with 10 years experience?

Recently, in a sales presentation by a prestigious recruiting management consulting firm, I asked the president of the firm about requests from clients that evidenced discrimination. He was quick to point out that discrimination on the part of his clients was nonexistent. In fact, he proudly reported that the contrary was true, that he was very often requested to submit applicants who were minorities and women. When questioned about job specifications that mentioned age, he hastily retreated and confessed that frequently the job specifications had age brackets attached to them, verbal requests, naturally, never in writing.

Sad to say, some of the worst offenders are personnel management people. Some time ago, an excellent personnel director was unemployed for almost a year here on Long Island. When he finally secured a job, he felt the reason it took so long to find employment was his age, which at the time was 50. He witnessed discrimination firsthand. Just a short time later he contacted me, after getting the job, and requested my help in locating a young recruiter, about 26 to 28 years of age, with a few years' experience. When I suggested a person of 55 years of age with 25 years of experience, willing to work for the salary he was offering, he was quick to reiterate his desire for a young person, of course no objection to a woman or a minority. Although these examples of discrimination are anecdotal, they are repeated daily. Discrimination is as insidious as hypertension or diabetes.

Older workers, in most cases, are being discriminated against by companies that are unaware that they are discriminating and, what is worse, employees are unaware that they are being discriminated against, because of the subtleties involved. When discrimination is not so subtle and is overt, the anger and response of individuals and groups of older employees increases, as evidenced by the fact that in the last 2 years or so, the government has brought 124 cases of age discrimination against such companies as Ford, Boeing, Chrysler, Pan American, United Airlines, Exxon, Shell, Du Pont, Westinghouse, and McDonnell-Douglas. Nearly $9 million have been paid out to some 2,000 employees by companies found guilty, including $250,000 paid to 72 employees at I.T.T. Some 400 other companies were brought to various courts in 1978 by individuals claiming discrimination. Probably a larger number of cases have been settled outside the judiciary system.

In a survey done recently, in which 4,500 people of all age groups participated, 80 percent felt that companies discriminate against the older workers. Interestingly enough, 97 percent of those surveyed who had an individual responsibility for hiring and promoting people felt the same way. Although there is an increasing awareness on the part of the individuals and companies in relation to discrimination on the basis of age, the awareness is momentary. That is, when a case of discrimination is made by an individual and brought to the company, it receives the attention that a leak in a factory window does. Fix the leak, and back to business as usual. Little thought is given to reviewing the causes of the alleged discrimination. Most employers are more likely to consider the applicant or the employee paranoid when age discrimination is brought up.

An industry mentality that young is good and older is bad results in a self-fulfilling prophecy. Older workers perceive their value and ability to be diminishing because that is the perception and expectation of management. This results in behavior on the part of some older workers which contributes to the myths about the older workers. In fact, studies have shown that only in the area of depression is there a significant difference between the younger and older worker. And that is not to say that younger people don't get depressed as often as older workers; rather, it takes longer for the older worker to recover from depression. Apparently he is not as resilient as his younger counterpart. Yet there are no significant differences in the ability to learn, absenteeism, or job performance. In fact, in a study of one large manufacturing company, in which layoffs were conducted on the basis of performance rather than seniority, and following the layoff of some 13,000 people on the basis of performance, there was an increase of eight years in the average age of the employee, from thirty-seven to forty-five years of age. That seems to indicate that there is a positive correlation between age and performance.

Nevertheless, the myths about the older worker persist, especially for the unemployed older worker. The discrimination that the older worker faces seems to be in direct proportion to his age. In a Ford Foundation study by Wilcox and Sobel, 4,000 workers were studied in six states. Two-thirds of the nearly 3,000 older workers had been laid off after long service with companies in comparatively well-paying jobs. When they finally found work again, the jobs that they found were the lowest paying and the least attractive in terms of prestige and status. This downward movement is evidenced by reports of median income by age. The median income of the 55 to 64 age group was substantially less than 45 to 54 age group,which, in turn, had a lower median income than the 35 to 44 age group.

There are further examples of myths and discrimination that only add to the weight of evidence already discussed to show the inadequacy of Congress, the Department of Labor, and industry. The two major questions to be asked are, what will industry do to resolve the problems of the middle-aged worker, and what can industry do?

Basically pragmatic by nature, industry will respond to the needs of the older worker, if it can be convinced that it is good business to do business with the older worker. Only a massive education and awareness program mounted by the government, exploding the myths and providing meaningful statistics and demographic information, can hope to convince industry to mount a voluntary program within their companies to protect the middle-aged and older worker. If this is marketed properly, industry is capable of a voluntary response to the problem. If the government fails to convince industry, or if industry fails to respond to the government's voluntary program, the conclusion, regrettably, will be the enactment yet of another affirmative action program. Industry will respond to the voluntary program as it has for other protected groups.

Addressing the second question, what can industry voluntarily do to resolve the problem, the following is offered as an industry model:

- Following a commitment from top management, promulgate a positive policy ensuring "a fair shake" for employees between the ages of 40 and 70.

- Make the policy statement known to all employees and mandate that the subject be a part of all supervisory development training programs within the company.

- Review all company personnel policies, practices, and benefits to determine if there are built-in prejudices not consistent with fair treatment. At a minimum, the review should include hiring, promotion and upgrading, career counseling, performance appraisals and training, compensation, termination, retirement, pensions and long-term disability, as well as life insurance and other benefit programs, and recreational and social programs.

- Based on the minimal available demographic data provided by the Department of Labor, perform a work-force composition utilization analysis. The Department of Labor Employment and Earnings Report which was put out in April 1979, indicates that 40 percent of the national work force is age 40 and over; 31 percent of the work force is age 45 and over. Although the Age Discrimination Employment Act provides protection for employees between the ages of 40 and 70, most of the difficulties for employees start at age 45. The work-force analysis of the company should be done both for age 40 and older and for 45 and older. The company's percent of total employees should be measured against a national work-force availability. In addition, the same analysis should be done by the various EEO-1 job categories of officials and managers, professionals, technicians, and so on. If underutilization is significant in any category, a further analysis should be performed to determine if one or more of the major departments within the company is the cause of the underutilization. A sampling of particular skills within the company should be subjected to the same utilization analysis. Trends from year to year should also be analyzed.

- The analysis should be done annually for new hires, terminations and promotions, training raises, recreational programs, etc., to complete the task.

- Special attention should be paid to an analysis of layoffs and discharges by age; after-hours training programs, supervisory and professional development programs; promotions into supervisory positions and within levels of supervisory positions.

- In most middle-to-large-size companies, most of the data required to do the utilization analysis are already contained in the computers; consequently the analysis is relatively simple and is neither particularly expensive nor time-consuming, especially after the initial program is designed.

- Finally, industry can ensure that the proper mechanism is set up within the company to ensure that any employee with an allegation of age discrimination can have his case reviewed objectively, and that a fair solution is provided.

In summary, there is probably more discrimination of an insidious nature inflicted upon the middle-aged and older worker than there is against any of our other protected classes in the United States today.

The Age Discrimination Employment Act has not adequately provided full protection for the older worker. Congress should consider a further revision of the Age Discrimination Employment Act to require the Department of Labor to initiate a voluntary program in industry. The failure of either the Department of Labor or industry would suggest still further revisions to the Age Discrimination Employment Act. Regrettably, such failure should result in Congress adopting an affirmative action provision within the Age Discrimination Employment Act.

Industry certainly has to consider setting up a voluntary program within companies before a mandated program is imposed upon them. Each company, at minimum, must have a commitment from top management to provide all employees with a written policy pertaining to the older worker. A thorough review of all the personnel policies should be made. The work-force utilization analysis should be made as a practical way to ensure that discrimination is not taking place within the organization.

A great deal of research material is available in the field of gerontology. However, much of the information has been generated for the sake of scholarly study. Too little of it has been directed in a simplified practical manner to affect the biggest single influence in the older employee's work life—his employer. It is a call to return to the use of the KISS principle-Keep It Simple Stupid. Further grants into gerontological research organizations should be directed toward studies of a practical nature that will influence industry to help the older worker.

DISCUSSION

This discussion was chaired by Daniel Knowles. Panelists were: Audrey H. Jones, Personnel Policies and Services Manager, Long Island Lighting Company; Peter Krajeski, Director of Personnel,

South Oaks Hospital; Peter Van Putten, Jr., Director of Personnel, Hazeltine Corporation; and William Voorhest, Special Assistant to the Chairman of the Board and President, and Director of Security and Corporate Services, Grumman Aerospace Corporation.

Audience:

Mr. Knowles, what is being done on a voluntary basis in industry at this time, if anything?

Mr. Knowles:

My perception of what is going on in industry is that very little is going on. Industry is basically pragmatic. To a large degree the government is setting priorities for industry. It certainly set the priority for affirmative action. The fact that there is not an affirmative-action program for the middle-aged and older worker or anything that is really positive being fostered by the government means you are going to get little response in a meaningful way from industry. When the pressure is applied by government, industry will respond. If you think industry is going to respond entirely out of the milk of human kindness, that is being naive.

Ms. Jones:

To follow up on that, two or three years ago a large company in New York City had a massive layoff of management people. Of the about 200 people who were discharged, most were the older, higher-paid employees, and the EEOC has finally gotten around to bringing a charge against them. The results of this in monetary back-pay payments may have some impact on what the rest of us do.

Audience:

When there is going to be a reduction in force, companies frequently sweeten the retirement program to encourage the older person to retire first. It seems to be a view of management and a view of employees to expect the older employee to move out.

Mr. Knowles:

I disagree with that. In this country we are going into a much more behavioral approach towards retirement. What we are doing is going in both directions at the same time. There is more and more need and desire on the part of employees to take earlier and earlier retirement. At the same time, people want to stay longer and longer. What we are really heading for in this country is more choice on the part of individuals to determine their own destiny in terms of retirement. Many people who want early retirement are not taking it for the sake of retiring, but for the prospect of going into a second career.

The more money you make and the better job you have, the more likely you are to be able to have a second career. I think there is a direct relationship between what your retirement income is, or what you earned in your first job and how much money you saved, and whether or not you are going to have the luxury of doing what you really want to do with your life. In terms of early-retirement incentives, what industry is doing is *not* telling people to get out; it is giving them an opportunity to do something with their lives that they really *want* to do. That is one of the reasons that there are early-retirement programs. That is why in the automobile industry, regardless of age, they have 30 years and out. Why? Because 30 years of putting the front right wheel on a car is an assault on people. I don't find the new directions in retirement incompatible at all. I think it is giving options and dignity to people.

Mr. Van Putten:

There is a misconception that if there is no mandatory retirement age, no one is ever going to leave. That creates a fear among employers, particularly in terms of telling old Charlie and old Sally, who really should have gotten a reasonable performance evaluation years ago that would have shown they were not performing up to par, that it is desirable for them to get out; so, of course, the easy way to do that is to create some sort of retirement situation.

I work for a company that does not have a mandatory retirement age. It is amazing how few people stay beyond their mid-60's. At the present time, with a base of about 2,800 employees, we have five or six employees who are in their 70's and I think we have one gentleman who is in his 80's. They are all very productive, and they are not being pushed out. Yet the majority of people still start leaving between the ages of 60 and 65. I think many are looking for a second career because I too believe, after working in an industry for 40 years, how many people actually achieve the level they want? Sometimes they do become nonproductive and complacent. The technology is changing very rapidly, and we have to find ways of making it interesting for people to stay. I don't see that we are forcing people out, I think we've reached a point where technological changes are happening so rapidly that people are finding that they are going to have to keep up more with the technological changes and/or find a second career.

Audience:

Is industry today making the prospective retirees aware of the opportunities available to them in their retirement?

Mr. Knowles:

Larger companies with more resources have initiated preretirement counseling programs. In my company, we are starting at age 55. All the people who will be 55 in a given year will be put through a program, as well as those who are 60 and 64. We bring them in with their spouses for an evening program. We give them a tape recorder and a series of tapes and a booklet to work on together at home for a six-week period. The program covers a great many topics pertaining to retirement, especially the area of financial planning for people who are 55. If you plan on retiring at age 65, then age 64 is not the time to start your financial planning. We then bring them back in to hear guest speakers with various degrees of expertise—someone from the medical department, the legal department, from Social Security, recreation, and so on. The major responsibility for a person's retirement lies with the person himself.

Audience:

I spoke to an employee in a large bank who was of retirement age, and he said they had a pre-retirement firm come in and give them some advice; and the advice they gave them was to tell them where they could buy houses cheaper than they are in this area. To me that is not a program.

Mr. Knowles:

Right, that is not a program. But where you are going to live is an important consideration. One of the most tragic things that people do in making mistakes about retirement is to sell their house and move to Florida, without testing it. I have seen an awful lot of people make that mistake. What they ought to do is rent here, and then rent in Florida or Arizona or where-have-you to make sure they are compatible with that area. After they have tested the area, then sell the house and buy another. One of the most important things about retirement is where you are going to live.

Ms. Jones:

We have pre-retirement seminars. We also do pre-retirement counseling for the husband and wife as a team, or the husband and daughter, or wife and son, or whoever happens to be able to come in. This is quite comprehensive.

Mr. Voorhest:

With inflation, I've noticed a lot of talk among our employees about fear of retirement. Right now, people are afraid to retire because they can't handle the economics.

Audience:

Many people are already retired and on fixed incomes. They find that they can't make it, and they want to go back to work but only on a part-time basis. How is industry responding to this? Are there shared work weeks, part-time jobs that can pay enough to supplement Social Security or a small retirement pension?

Mr. Knowles:

Some years ago I wrote a letter to all of our retired employees. I asked how many of them would be interested in coming back to work in some capacity, either part-time, on call, or on a temporary basis. More than 50 percent indicated that they would be interested in considering some form of employment. We have brought those people back as either consultants or job-shoppers, because to bring them back as employees would interfere with their pension.

Mr. Krajeski:

If your company has a tuition assistance or training reimbursement program for employees who are attending college, certainly making that available to older workers as an opportunity to create a second career should be part of your thinking.

Audience:

I'd like to respond to the question about the retired employee who can't make it on his pension. I believe that industry is moving towards adjusting pension plans based on the inflationary spiral. Our company just gave pensioners an increase of 16 percent to make adjustments for inflation. I think that we are going to find that large corporations are going to move in this direction.

Mr. Knowles:

For over 10 years our pension plan has had a cost-of-living escalator built into it to offer some protection.

Audience:

It is heartening to hear that industry is taking care of its own, but what about the older employee who is not on a pension, who is hanging in there on Social Security, and can't afford to work full-time without losing some of that, and just wants to work part-time? Are there any opportunities to come into industry on a part-time or a job-shared basis?

Mr. Knowles:

I don't think there are any statistics that would say how many jobs like that are available. It is a very individual thing. What I am saying and keep repeating is that the government has got to be the initiator for this type of thing. I don't necessarily mean everything being done through legislation, but if nothing else, an education program. They are spinning their wheels down there. They get over-sophisticated, and they are not providing practical, meaningful programs.

Mr. Krajeski:

I recognize the need for government pressure on industry to get us to comply, but at the same time I don't see why we can't go a little further in our own recognition of social problems, recognition of the importance of older workers, and recognition of the special skills and dedication they can bring to us.

Mr. Voorhest:

I am going to say it very simply; it just won't work.

Mr. Knowles:

The very fact that South Oaks Hospital hosts a seminar tells you something about social conscience. How many companies do you know that are sponsoring programs like this?

Mr. Krajeski:

Isn't there a lot we can do, as individuals, without top management approval and policies?

Mr. Knowles:

It is not going to be done. There are 24 million Americans in this country over age 65. If we had an audience of nothing but personnel directors throughout the United States, maybe we could do something. Yes, each of us doing our own little thing will help, but it is shoveling sand against the tide.

Mr. Voorhest:

Industry's bottom line is profit. They will not do anything unless it is profit-motivated. You must put teeth in the laws to make it happen. *Then* it will happen.

Mr. Krajeski:

I've read a lot about the cost savings involved with the older worker because that worker comes to work on a more regular basis than the younger worker. We have a program called a Low Sick Time Bonus Plan. Last year 108 people received that bonus, and 80 percent of those people were over age 40. Of the people who never missed a day's work last year, 84 percent were over age 40. There is also less turnover, we know. This all adds up to a real cost benefit.

Mr. Voorhest:

We care about people at Grumman, but for the average industry all that counts is the bottom line. They are not educated enough to know that what you say is true.

Audience:

A few years ago, the government mandated the hiring of minorities and women. I don't think industry has found that this has been unprofitable. In fact it is very profitable, and I am sure that if there was a law that mandated the hiring of older people, industry would suddenly find that is profitable.

Mr. Knowles:

Right on, that is what we have been saying.

Audience:

The question might well be asked why doesn't the government put the middle-aged and aged in the affirmative-action category? The answer is that, psychologically speaking, the people who have the power in the government to do that, do not advocate the rights of the middle-aged and the aged. They don't want to recognize the fact that they themselves are going to get into that category. This is a psychological quirk that they have.

Mr. Knowles:

There is no question that the priorities for the older and middle-aged worker are not equivalent to the priorities that have been set for other protected groups. If you are ever in Washington, go into the House and just walk by the offices of the various members of Congress and look at the age of the staff people. You will find the average age is about 28. That is where the Pepsi Generation is. Not the members of the House, but the staffs.

Audience:

I want to talk about the schools for a moment. There is the thinking that retirement solves a lot of problems and schools often use retirement as an "easy" method of firing, or lowering of budgets, as well as a performance criterion.

Mr. Knowles:

In our school systems on Long Island, many teachers leave off their credentials when they apply for jobs. They leave off their work beyond the master's degree because they feel they are going to be discriminated against by being qualified. Just look at your own school districts and see who gets the few jobs that are available. Young kids coming right out. The schools think they are getting a bargain. In this life you get what you pay for. If you hire somebody for $8,000 you get $8,000 worth of person. If you hire somebody for $18,000, you are going to get $18,000 worth of person, all things being equal. Sure, there are exceptions but basically you pay for what you get, you get what you pay for.

Mr. Krajeski:

There is a concept in personnel about staying away from people who made more money on their last job. We have to think about the people who are, for one reason or another, out of work who were making high salaries, but who are willing to work for less.

Audience:

As an employee stays on beyond age 65, for various reasons he may become less productive in the eyes of the company. Are these companies giving thought to training programs, to make these employees more valuable to the company?

Mr. Knowles:

I think what you said has some small grain of truth. As people get older they need to be retrained. But, by and large, I reject the premise. I don't think that there is a diminishing of ability, brain power, or overall performance because of age. In my talk I cited the case of a company that laid off 13,000 people on the basis of performance, and the average age went from 37 to 45. That runs counter to what you are saying. There *should* be a relationship between age and performance. The older you get, theoretically, the better you should get; recognizing the fact that there is a difference between a person who has 20 year's experience and a person who has one year's experience, 20 times over. I don't think that the major issue is a need for retraining older workers.

Ms. Jones:

I agree with this, but I think there is a correlation between the older worker and stagnation. Most of the people who are in our big companies on Long Island came out here after World War II. They are now reaching upper middle age. They have been in the same jobs for a long, long time. We are now getting into the whole area of the baby-boom people who are approaching middle age. This is going to be another big group of people who will be in the work force for the next 30 to 35 years. We have got to rethink management, development, job rotations, all kinds of different things. If we don't have promotional opportunities, we are going to have to find other ways to keep people from stagnating. No matter what the age of the person, the freedom from depression is known to correlate directly with increased job skills. As you give people more to do; new things to learn, no matter what their age, they become more capable and more able to cope with what is going on around them.

Audience:

Regarding the comment about people being laid off because of lack of productivity, I don't think very many companies today have that luxury, because a good many companies are governed by union contracts, and workers are laid off according to seniority, not productivity. Recently my company laid off everybody with up to 10 years of service. Naturally, the age of the average employee was increased tremendously. For those of us who are pretty hard-nosed, when we get down to that bottom-line figure, we ask ourselves what is the attitude of an employee toward his job when that individual gets to an age of, say, 55 to 65, and has been working for a corporation for 30, 35 years. How do we motivate that old group to be as productive as they were 25 years ago? That is a big problem today. I think that industry will have to do something to motivate these people.

Mr. Van Putten:

Those in the personnel field, and, it is hoped, those whom we are trying to train in management, are becoming more aware that we have to care more about people with respect to career development and personal growth. It has taken a long time for us to get to this point, but we are beoming much more aware of people as individuals, without the tags that we have attached in the past, such as age, race, sex, and so on. In the future, when we go into career-development programs, we are going to be talking to a person as a person, not as an age, not as a sex, not as a minority member. We do have a lot of hang-ups with regard to whom we hire and what we look for. A young supervisor may want only younger people. A person who graduated from a certain school, probably has other people with him from that school. We all have been taught to favor associations, clubs, unions, and other ties. We have to educate people to get rid of these hang-ups.

Mr. Voorhest:

I have been in Grumman Corporation for 39 years. I hear a lot of people say, boy, the good old days were really great. I think the good old days were really bad, because I remember when you were lucky to get a "Good morning" out of the foreman. The individual didn't really count that much. Today we have a personal department; we have so much more than we had before. The world is getting better for the worker.

Audience:

I agree. There are people like me, who are young, who are holding administrative positions, and who have come here today on our own because we are interested in hiring older people. So, Mr. Knowles, you shouldn't be so hard on the young.

Mr. Knowles:

It is not being hard on youth as much as it is being pro-middle-age and older worker. I don't think you need a special program for youth; there are hundreds of those programs all over. There are no programs for the middle-aged and older worker. I really am not negative on young people. You need each band of the age spectrum. They each have something to contribute. Young people bring a vitality; older people bring a wisdom. The older people get a little more sophisticated in how they handle their jobs, and younger people have a tendency to bull their way through. The go on energy rather than experience.

Mr. Voorhest:

We can't be hard on younger people, because what we want to do is make use of all people.

Mr. Knowles:

It is not the young people who discriminate against middle-aged and older people, it is the middle-aged and older people who discriminate against middle-aged and older people. Most young people are not in a position to do it.

Audience:

As personnel administrators, do you encounter any significantly different psychological or mental health problems associated with anxiety about aging or impending retirement? We seem to put all people in one classification—30 to 40, 40 to 50, 50 to 60. Older people are entirely different, and the 40-year-old man might be older than the 70-year-old man. People are different, their needs are different, and you have to have different programs for each one.

Audience:

A lot of people want to retire because they feel the pressures of the job. But they would like to continue working, so they take advantage of retirement hoping that they are going to get a second career. Sometimes this does not materialize; they can't get employment, or frequently they will take a lower-level job. Is there any way of considering a reshuffling within the organization? The thought of stepping down within their own organization is usually not even considered. This is an important area. Why leave the company where you feel at home if you would be willing to step down? This would require education and a change of attitude on the part of all people.

Ms. Jones:

Demotion within your own company, whether it is by choice or not, is a difficult thing. I don't know anybody who has accepted it gracefully or easily. Co-workers are not always that kind. No matter how much you proclaim that the job change was by choice, they are always going to say, oh, he or she just couldn't cut it.

Audience:

I realize that, but we are talking about the need for a whole new approach to this concept.

Ms. Jones:

We have done it, not by the workers' choice, but by our own necessity. People who crack under the pressure or strain of a new job are put in another category. We also do it quite frequently with people who are physically unable to do hard work.

Mr. Krajeski:

Employees should have the option to accept voluntarily different types of jobs within the organization, understanding that there could be loss of pay, and pension complications. Our plan pays a pension based on the best five years of your last 10 years of employment. If in your last 10 years of employment, you switch down to a lower-paying job that would not be to your benefit, pension plans have to be evaluated. I know of a physically disabled person who realized he had a serious physical illness and chose to step down from a demanding position to a less demanding one. It worked out very successfully. We should have these kinds of options available.

Audience:

I have spent a great deal of time in the last couple of years studying and doing research in gerontology, and the training and development of the older worker. You are all talking about the needs that management has, that the worker has. Is business and industry ready for me to come in and get something done, or is it all talk?

Mr. Knowles:

No, we are not ready for you to come in, and yes, it is a lot of talk. American industry is not ready because there is no pressure on them to do this.

Audience:

You still feel the pressure has to come from government?

Mr. Knowles:

It is not going to be self-generated. I would advise you to put the heat on your Congressman to do something to give equal consideration to the middle-aged and older workers as we give to other protected groups—pure and simple.

Audience:

Do you think with the voting population now to be over age 52, social policies would necessarily be shaped to favor the voting population?

Mr. Knowles:

No. Unless you have a problem, you don't have the motivation to get interested in it. The person who is middle-aged who is discriminating against another middle-aged person, doesn't think of it as the problem of the person whom he is discriminating against. The middle-aged and older workers in this country have not been incensed enough to do something.

Mr. Krajeski:

I think there will be some pressures very shortly because of the effect of the decreasing birth rate. Industry right now is pretty fat and happy; we have a lot of people applying for jobs. But in a very short time we should begin to feel the pressure of the decreasing abundance of workers, with a resulting change in our opinions about retirees. If the government doesn't eliminate the mandatory retirement age, industry will change it, I am sure, out of necessity for the need of available labor. We will want people to work longer. People are living longer now, and people are getting healthier. I think industry will be changing its attitudes about older workers within a short period of time.

Audience:

I am hearing two views. One is that businesses will act when government makes them. The other is that businesses might act if they could be convinced it is good business. What kind of statistics would it take to convince you that it is good business?

Mr. Knowles:

Let's talk about the demographics first of all. I said earlier that if you ask any individual company whether they discriminate against middle-aged and older workers, they rise up with indignation. Then you ask them, what percentage of your work force is middle-aged and older, and they look at you blankly. So the first thing is knowing the makeup of your own company. Most companies don't know their own age makeup.

The second thing is, in order to determine whether or not in a global or universal way you are discriminating, you have got to have data about the availability of the work force. The Department of Labor has done a miserable job in providing that kind of data. What they have are gross figures, the percentage of the work force that is over 40, that kind of figure. That doesn't necessarily mean that that is the percentage of people who are in a professional category, or a craftsman category; it doesn't break down as to the availability of carpenters, assemblers, riveters, electronic technicians, and so on. So to do a halfway decent analysis, you have got to have the demographics—not only in the entire country, but in your own company—to see how your company matches up with the availability of people in the work force. Demographics, number one.

Number two, get rid of the old myths—you can't teach an old dog new tricks, absenteeism is higher among older workers—which are not true. Just look at the research. All the psychological and physiological studies indicate that there is no significant difference that is going to prevent people from being able to work. You are not going to have an eighty-three-year-old test pilot, but there are relatively few jobs in industry that have any relationship to age. We have to explode this kind of misconception about middle-aged and older workers. The Department of Labor saw fit to do it for women. They have done a reasonable, succinct job of exploding myths about women—that women are just working at second jobs to have frills, and send their children through college. They have analyzed what percentage of women are running households, and so on. This has not been done by the Department of Labor for the middle-aged and older worker.

Audience:

I went to a business library and tried to get some information about the insurance coverage offered by different companies. How accessible is that kind of information for purpose of study?

Mr. Van Putten:

Insurance companies have tons of that. That is what they base their livelihood on.

Mr. Knowles:

That is one of the other smokescreens that is put up: that it is not profitable to hire middle-aged and older workers because the cost is greater for pensions, and so on. Most companies couldn't even identify those costs in any way, shape, or form. It is a stereotyped view. I dare say that probably only one in a million companies in the United

States has ever done a real in-depth analysis of insurance costs in relation to age in their company. But even if the older worker did cost more, young people cost the company even more in terms of training, and in terms of absenteeism. What difference does it make what a person is absent for? If they are absent due to depression because they are older, what is the effective difference from the case of some young person who is out because of a love affair? It is still absenteeism. The causes are different, but not the net result, and that is what counts for the company.

Mr. Krajeski:

One source I use all the time is the American Management Association research library. If your corporation is a member you simply call them and they will research any number of areas for you.

Mr. Knowles:

What I am talking about does not require a high degree of sophistication. We are talking about some very simple, basic management-type information. Don't load down your business people with the fantastic in-depth studies that have been done. They are not interested in that. They are interested in the bottom-line kind of information. I am not talking about putting out an encyclopedia: I am talking about a small booklet of information. That is what business people would be responsive to.

Mr. Van Putten:

What is the mandatory retirement age at South Oaks?

Mr. Krajeski:

We don't have a mandatory age. We have a guideline of age 70, but with department-head approval you can extend that with no problem. Basically, the question is asked of all department heads, do you have a person who is still performing adequately? We have a number of people over age 70.

Mr. Van Putten:

What is the mandatory retirement age at LILCO?

Ms. Jones:

Seventy.

Mr. Knowles:

Seventy at Grumman.

Mr. Van Putten:

You could talk to a lot of organizations until you are blue in the face, but as long as there is an age bracket to stick to they are going to stay with it. Will they make exceptions? Yes they will, for the chairman of the board or some special person.

Mr. Voorhest:

When we went to Iran with 400 employees and their families, the average age of those employees was 43 to 45. The most adaptable people with the least attrition on the whole program were that age group. If you ever have a situation where you have to go to a remote part of a country, live off the economy, and have no communications, send your older worker.

Ms. Jones:

We don't have a high turnover rate. We have the opposite problem. Our turnover rate is somewhere between 3 percent and 4 percent and we do have many people who have 40 and 45 years service when they retire. Our problem is that half the company is going to leave within the next 10 years. What I am trying to do is to make sure that we keep enough of the younger middle-aged—35 to 45—so that they will be ready to take over these spots.

We are still finding that early retirements before the age of 65 outweigh retirement at 65 by about two to one.

Mr. Knowles:

One of the other copouts, I think, is that the company says it wants younger people because they will stay and make their career there. Well, doing a little analysis in our own company, I found that the average person who retires is 62 years and five months old and has been with the company 22 ½ years. That means you have no problem when you hire people in their 40's, they are going to stay with you. The problem with younger people, not again to pick on them, is that you have to put three creative development specialists on their tail to keep them self-actualized. By the time a person is 45 or 50, he understands something—he is not going to be president. At 25 you don't know that.

Audience:

I teach gerontology, and do training and developing, and I am always telling everybody that it is terrific to get old. Now I am getting very depressed. I am 39 years old and you are talking about people reaching middle age at 35. I would like to know what the market is for people who are 40 and over who are coming into new careers. I didn't feel old until today.

Mr. Knowles:

Well, you have one thing going for you. You are a woman. We have affirmative action programs in companies for women. But if you were a man...

Ms. Jones:

I see a lot of women in the empty-nest age group. Former teachers who try to go back into the job market are having a great deal of difficulty because the skills they are offering are not the skills that are needed. If people are willing to go back and get the skills that are needed, they will find a job because many are going unfilled. We can't keep programmers, for example. We would love to get women engineers or women with any kind of math or science skills.

Mr. Krajeski:

We really don't care what you are today—man or woman, young or old—when you present yourself as an applicant. There are guidelines of course, but really the question has to remain, are you qualified for the position you are applying for?

Audience:

You look for people with particular skills, but very often in middle-aged their skill is peculiar to their own company, and is of little benefit to anyone else. Yet they feel it would be demeaning to take a lesser position.

Ms. Jones:

I believe in the theory of transferable skills. I have made three complete career changes. I started out as a biochemical research technician, stayed home for six years, went back to work and back to school in marine biology, and I am now in personnel. Each of these was a progression. I really belonged in personnel from the beginning.

Mr. Van Putten:

All of us have to learn to deal with the word *change*. Change of job, change of marital status, change of family composition. I believe that the most difficult and painful task an individual ever faces is job hunting. The feeling of rejection can be overpowering.

The same thing applies to people as they get into a retirement situation; it is change again—a change of life style, the change of learning to live in a new way. We have to learn to cope better with change.

Mr. Krajeski:

I became familiar with the problem of the older worker only recently. When I was assigned to this panel I did some research and reading. I could not believe what is happening to the unemployed older worker. I couldn't believe that it takes upwards of a year for a person who is over age 45 or 50 to find a position, and in many cases it is not a position paying the salary that was made before. In 20 percent of these cases, it takes longer than a year. Marriages are disrupted, savings expended.

Mr. Jones:

One of the things that companies are considering, if they can afford it, is outplacement for older people. When a person is terminated from the job, usually not for poor performance but for bad fit, or retrenchment, the company, in lieu of severance, sends them to an outplacement firm. The company pays the fee which is usually 15 percent of the person's salary. These people then teach the candidate how to go about looking for a job. We have used this with great success in a few cases. In fact, people who were outplaced got better jobs than they had before.

Audience:

Do the outplacement firms help people who are not from within the company?

Ms. Jones:

Some do. The fee, in that kind of situation, would have to be determined by the level of job which is sought. If you are looking for a $30,000 job, it would be 15 percent of $30,000. But primarily they are geared for helping industry to help their current employees.

Mr. Van Putten:

I have been in the personnel field for almost 20 years and I, too, went through a career change from engineering into personnel. I am very pleased with the profession because 20 years ago, or even 10 years ago, there were not many personnel people who participated in these kinds of activities, or had these kinds of concerns. I hope we can leave you with a note of optimism, that we are trying. But we can't do it alone, there has got to be more support. You have got to talk to your legislators, because that is what makes it happen. It isn't just us. We can't do the entire job. It needs the people to make it happen, and that's you as well as us.

Mr. Knowles:

I detect an antagonistic situation between industry and government, especially in the area of the affirmative action programs that we do have. So I am not looking forward to seeing an affirmative action program for the middle-aged and older worker. It is too bad that in this country we should need them, but we do. It seems to me that we have set up an awful situation between the compliance agencies that review the affirmative action programs or review discrimination cases. You have relatively young lawyers from second-rate schools who are the people responsible in Washington for drafting legislation. Don't ever think your Congressman is drafting legislation. It is people you and I have never heard of who are coming up with the laws. These people with their missionary zeal project their own personal prejudices and biases, and we get into the bully syndrome—the big company picking on the little employee. More time and more money and more resources to perpetuate a bad relationship between government and industry in general. It is about time that government and industry started to work together to improve the quality of life for *all* people in this country.

Chapter 3

ORGANIZED LABOR—QUALITY OF LIFE AND THE AGING WORKER

*John J. McManus**

During the past 10 years, the experience of the AFL-CIO Department of Community Services has revealed that the aging worker is a subject accorded little interest by workers of any age. This includes both international and national unions that comprise the AFL-CIO federation, as well as social agencies, other organizations, and individuals with whom we come in contact. It is as though the aged are an alien race to which the young will never belong.

In the AFL-CIO Department of Community Services, we are constantly revising pamphlets on all phases of community services, and periodically running out of copies because of a steady distribution. But this is not so with our pamphlet on pre-retirement and retirement planning. The initial limited printing of this pamphlet was

*Mr. McManus is Assistant Director of the AFL-CIO Department of Community Services in Washington, D.C.

Prior to joining the AFL-CIO, Mr. McManus served as the first Executive Director of the United Fund of Long Island, as Commissioner of Public Welfare and Chairman of the Board of Public Welfare in Nassau County, New York, and as the first Executive Director of the Health and Welfare Council in Nassau County. He currently serves on the Executive Committee and Board of the American Health Planning Association.

Mr. McManus received his Master of Social Service degree from Adelphi University.

18 years ago—and we have yet to run out of copies, or to receive inquiries that would motivate us to prepare a new model.

Because of this lack of response, in 1977 the AFL-CIO Department of Community Services sponsored an all-day meeting on pre-retirement planning—and less than a dozen out of 104 international-national unions attended. There have been no requests for a follow-up, and evidently no one wanted to know of the proceedings.

I suggest to you, as students of human behavior, that aging, as a term, is repulsive to us as individuals. It is the *other* worker—she's aging, notice all that gray hair and those facial wrinkles—*she* should get into pre-retirement planning, but not me. I may be older than that worker, but I'm not aging as fast. Go talk to her, but I'm O.K.

Much of the philosophy in this paper should be credited to a physician, Siegmund H. May, M.D., formerly Medical Director of the A. Holly Patterson Home in Uniondale, Long Island. In 1964 Dr. May brought to this 900-bed geriatric institution a form of responsive and responsible patient care that is still with us today. In his book, *The Crowning Years*,[1] he comments that an ancient Greek philosopher advised his people to die young, but as late as possible. Dr. May's insights are so perceptive as to be worth an extended quote:

> The glowing autumn of life we all wish for is not a bliss granted by lucky genes, or by fortuitous circumstances alone. It is, preeminently, a reward bestowed on those who earn it—by foresight and forethought. We must not leave the advent of our later years to chance.
>
> Evidence is mounting that the many predicaments of the aging process befall us all, with only slight variations. The difference of the outcome is that some of us can tolerate them and live with them for decades without suffering great hardship. Adjustability is the secret. Besides strength and determination, it requires education and training. Learning the art of growing old should be one of the great accomplishments of our time.
>
> New and important ideas concerning age have recently occupied the forefront of medical thinking. However, since it is in the nature of science that the ways to the truth converge from many directions, not all those ideas are purely in the realm of medicine. We now know that growth in age is influenced and altered not only by physical conditions within us, but probably just as much by the happenings of the world around us.

As desirable as prolongation of life may seem, it does not in itself constitute a blessing. Unless we cherish the gift of the extra years and use them wisely, they may become surplus years, a nostalgic postscript. Life extension should be and can be life expansion, a sounder, richer, and fuller experience than we knew when we were busy earning a living and rearing a family. To make aging a career is everybody's prerogative. Anybody can start constructive planning for it at any time. But, by and large the earlier one begins the greater are the chances of success.

The art of living is the cultivation of our potentials. It is a commitment to ourselves to control circumstances in order to bring about the best physical and mental health in us. It is a commitment to human values. In the art of aging the art of living reaches its highest level.

In what ways, therefore, is the aging worker different from other human beings? The aging worker can certainly perform effectively—even maintaining the basic productivity requirements of management. On the other hand, the aging worker, while performing adequately in the shop, can at the same time become fearfully discouraged and even engage in self-pity. It is not difficult to anticipate the effects of work-place stress on a worker, whether it is peer pressure, high—and perhaps unrealistic—personal standards of achievement, management-induced stress, or a combination of all these factors. Nevertheless, at age 36 a worker is classified as "aging" by Federal guidelines. At age 45 a worker might therefore be considered "over the hill," and at 55, a new senior citizen. One of the most distressing trends of life in the United States is the gradual devaluation of older people.

Not so, we inwardly object. That may be true for others, not for me, not for us. And yet the threat gets through to us all.

"Quality of life" and the aging worker are not, after all, incompatible entities, at the chronological age benchmarks of 36, 45, 55, or 75. Professional medicine has kept us living longer, and at the same time technology has made us sooner obsolete.

The good life, or the quality of life, is really achieved by the stimulation of interests. The ability to break with fixed habits can be a rewarding achievement in aging, and through the process of aging, lead to revitalization. The bottom line should say to us all that it is better to fight age than accept it.

The general slowing down in old age, the reduced excitability and irritability, as well as the release from the push and shove of competition, can regenerate the gaiety and happiness that accompanied our early carefree years.

For purposes of preparing this paper we turned to the National Council of Senior Citizens, with the question: "What three things would you specify as important to quality of life for the elderly?" Here are those three things:

1) A healthy economy, providing job opportunities for those of retirement age who still wish to work, and to generate the tax flow the Federal government needs to fund adequate assistance/service programs for the elderly.

2) National Health Security Insurance with good coverage for the elderly.

3) More specialized service/support facilities for older women to overcome their extraordinary isolation, particularly after their spouses die. The program focus needs to be on emotional interests and personal sustenance, not just meals and television.

Today, a worker's thoughts about aging—particularly where a collective bargaining agreement is in effect—highlight economic security and independence. We know that one out of every four Americans 65 or over lives at or below the poverty line, and that job discrimination against the aged, and increasingly against the middle-aged, is already a fact of U.S. life. While nearly 40 percent of the long-term unemployed are over age 45, only 10 percent of Federal retraining programs are devoted to men of that age. It is often difficult for older people to get bank loans, home mortgages, or automobile insurance. With the chaos that now exists in our national economy, with a dollar that is lighter than air, the aging worker is prone to ever-increasing economic tragedies. However, I wish to propose that in addition to the increasing benefit and assurances of collective-bargaining agreements, a full program of Community Services Activities holds considerable long-range value to the retired or retiring worker, and to our American society.

What do I suggest in the way of improving the quality of life for the aging worker through Community Service Activities?

A) An arts-educational-cultural program that will involve the worker long before becoming retired. Programs of this kind, when used in nursing homes, bring great personal satisfaction. But why wait for a nursing home to introduce us to creative, *fun* activities? Our great, former President of the AFL-CIO, George Meany, took up painting-by-numbers and developed an individual style that was remarkably artistic. President Meany began his art pursuit in later life, well before retirement, and he found it highly rewarding as a personal achievement.

B) Becoming active in more than one charitable organization—taking part in decision-making and in carrying out the services offered by the agency. In particular, a local United Labor Agency is an excellent location for a member of organized labor to set out to meet new acquaintances and form new personal coalitions. There are 24 United Labor Agencies now in operation, and one is right here on Long Island.

C) Involve our local and national unions in retirement planning, initiated five or 10 years prior to actual retirement, where none exists. Bring to our members information on the effect of inflation on retirement security, and the need for more careful retirement planning. The following retirement planning areas, developed by the National Council on the Aging, should be included in this context for workers and their spouses:
   1) Life-style planning
   2) Financial planning
   3) Leisure time
   4) Interpersonal relations
   5) Living arrangements
   6) Community services
   7) New careers in retirement
   8) Health

D) Get involved in one key area of political activity, collaborating with other concerned citizens, in a coalition designed to make certain that your best interests and those of your community are adequately represented and implemented properly.

The message that is to be shared and studied is that learning the art of growing old should be, and can be, one of our great personal achievements. Dr. Siegmund May, you will recall, gave us this companion message: "In the art of aging the art of living reaches its highest level."

DISCUSSION

Panelists for this discussion were: William J. Bolch, President, Mutuel Ticket Agents Union Local 23293; Eleanor Litwak, Director, Retirees Program, District Council 37 American Federation of State, County and Municipal Employees, AFL-CIO; Alexander Stieglitz, Executive Chairman, Air Transport Lodge 1056, International Association of Machinists and Aerospace Workers; and Charles Winick, Ph.D., Technical Consultant to the Central Labor Rehabilitation Council of New York.

Mr. Stieglitz:

I am affiliated with the International Association of Machinists, Local Lodge 1056. We represent Trans World Airlines at JFK International Airport, and we have approximately 2,800 members. We recently set up a pre-retirement seminar for our people—a six-week session—and we covered various aspects of retirement, including financial budgeting, estate planning, nutrition and health, leisure time and volunteer work, employment after retirement, and educational options. The last session covered company options: in this session we discussed our company's benefits, and how we are looking into changing the pension plan to include a cost-of-living addendum.

Mr. Bolch:

According to Federal guidelines, when you reach age 36, you are classified as aging. At age 45, you are over the hill, and at age 55, you are a senior citizen. I guess our union is a maverick. We have approximately 600 active employees at the present time, and it is interesting to note that 343 of these 600—more than half—are senior citizens, according to government standards: they are all over the age of 55. And 270, or 48 percent, of our mutuel clerks are over the age of 60. We believe in keeping everyone working. There are 183 mutuel clerks over the age of 65, I guess in the government's eyes they must be considered decrepit. Lastly, 105 of our 600 clerks are over the age of 70. I am talking about people actively working—that's 18 percent of my union over the age of 70. We have two clerks who handle thousands and thousands of dollars at the $50 window—one is 85 and the other is 84. A 70-year-old mutuel clerk just received an award for outstanding service; he has worked for 28 years without missing a single night of work. We have two clerks, each 90 years old, still working. They sit and check tickets. Our union believes in keeping the aging employee working.

Mr. Winick:

A Central Labor Council is a conglomerate of labor unions in a particular area. This organization works to achieve political, social, and welfare goals. New York City is a strong labor town, and its Central Labor Rehabilitation Council is part of the larger Central Labor Council. The Rehabilitation Council, as the health and welfare arm of approximately 600 local unions, provides a variety of services. Those local unions have a membership of about 1,600,000.

The Central Rehabilitation Council has a committee on pre-retirement and post-retirement which I have been working with for some time. We know how central an occupation is to a person's sense of worth and identity, and how a good deal of that individual's identity may be diminished when he or she retires. However, the union affiliation a person has is something that never diminishes. It always remains. The union provides a feeling of collegiality, an anchorage, and a sense of being a member of a large and very special kind of extended family. Retirement programs of many of the large unions are geared to maintain this feeling of cooperation and collegiality by having members and retirees do things together.

It is hard to generalize about unions. The nature of their leadership is crucial, as is the age at which retirement is encouraged or enabled. There are a number of items that are common to many union programs: food-stamp counseling; how to handle disabilities; financial assistance; meetings and lectures; educational programs; health and nutrition information; budgeting advice; newsletters; trips; discounts for merchandise; and opportunities for retirees to display their hobby handiworks.

Many unions have a vigorous legislative program because letters from retirees have just as much weight as letters from employees. Some unions are able to arrange for programs related to retirement during work hours: programs for people five years from retirement, three years, and finally one year away.

The Central Labor Council has also been asked about jobs for persons who have retired. We were able to negotiate with the Food Stamp office in New York City for part-time employment for a substantial number of retirees who would work as outreach persons to advise about stamp requirements. This is an example of constructive activity for which the participants are paid. There were a number of foundations in the New York area which had money available specifically to fund socially constructive projects for retirees.

Maybe 15 years ago we would have been discussing what is being done for older workers in terms of a very limited range of activities. Today there is a much wider range, and the growing emphasis is on preparing the person to face retirement, and helping that person to develop interests and follow a constructive path after retirement. Pre-retirement planning to enable a person to function effectively and creatively once retirement comes is the largest movement I see in union programs.

Ms. Litwak:

District Council 37 is the largest Municipal Employees Union in New York City. We bargain for 110,000 city employees. We have 24,000 known retirees, 16,000 of whom belong to our Retirees Association. Some unions permit their retirees active participation; ours doesn't. Therefore the Retirees Association was established to funnel retired members into an association of their own. Within the last three years, there has been a virtual revolution among the retirees, and their presence and visibility have become much stronger, far more focused, and wield greater impact. The most dramatic example of that impact is that upon the retirees' request, a cost-of-living adjustment in their pension stands as a primary item on the negotiating list.

Our union, too, has a substantial package of health and welfare benefits. We have very substantial educational benefits for active members and for retired members as well. For the retired, for instance, we have programs that take the participant in any direction, including a degree-granting college, high-school equivalency courses, classes in skills-upgrading including shorthand and graphics, and classes in literature, Shakespeare, and opera, which are very well attended. We also have programs in arts and crafts, folk dancing, and bridge.

Still, I have yet to find a pre-retirement package that I think is very good. I think they are superficial; they tend to be aimed at the middle classes. Our union is 65 percent female, 50 percent black and Hispanic, and about 60 percent of our members make less than $10,000 a year, which is below poverty level. I have never seen a pre-retirement package that really addresses itself to the needs of what I call the poor working class. My concern for this group has led me to broader considerations: is it possible, indeed, five years before you finish working, to plan for retirement? I say no. Nobody is interested. How do we engender interest? How do we get people to worry about the fact that they are indeed going to approach old age? It is not terribly hard to get them involved in the computation of the pension plus Social Security. They are always worried about bread-and-butter issues. But it is very hard to get people interested in pre-retirement planning once you go beyond actual dollars and cents.

I would like to suggest that we begin to think that preparation for retirement starts the day you enter the work force. Does that sound crazy? Those who go to work at age 16, 22, 25, should begin to think about retirement, and the way they should begin to think about it is by belonging to a network, a support group. Large-scale organizations that have access to people, such as labor unions and industries, must begin to deal with life-cycle issues in a network. What to talk about to a group of people in their 20's? The issues that affect this age group are the problems between the sexes, marriage, and children. Begin talking to them about these subjects. Begin talking at a very early age about the issues crucial at that given point in their life

cycle. Set up groups that discuss such issues, because this has a sociological, psychological meaning. In old age, one of the greatest
problems is aloneness. And by building and belonging to a support
group, when they enter the work force, means that people will be
prepared to open up to others in various crisis points of their life—including retirement. When the retirement years become imminent,
the habit of discussing personal fears and anxieties will have become
ingrained. A discussion about what you are going to do with your life
once you leave the workplace will come more naturally, have more
significance.

Retirement is no longer a joy to look forward to. It is a time of
deprivation, fear, aloneness. Develop a support group that goes with
you through crises of your life, and at the time you are about to retire,
that support group will be there to help.

Audience:

Your point about networks and developing peer groups at a
younger age is a good one. However, with the mobility of people and
the fact that most people don't stay in the same job for 30 years, how
do you do that if you change locations or change jobs?

Ms. Litwak:

I think that entry into the network can occur at almost any point.
We are a mobile society, but I don't think this presents an insurmountable problem. If a person who is on a worksite for one or
two years is welcomed in, then a service has been done to that worker,
whether that worker enters at 20 or at 40 or if he or she is lucky,
enters at 50. I see this as an ongoing flexible process.

Enlightened industry is good about release time; pre-retirement
groups normally will meet on industry time. The city does not give us
release time, so we hold pre-retirement sessions on Saturdays. We
have had very high response rates, but we can't do anything in one
day; you can't begin to touch, except in the most superficial manner,
upon the issues that will face one on retirement.

We have a support group of retirees, called, "Not to be Alone," made up of widows and widowers. As it has grown, we have brought in other single persons as well. They get together on weekends, on holidays, they are together at the loneliest times. They meet weekly at the union hall. This model works, at least for us in this one particular instance. I would like to know what the unions are doing, since you have much more immediate impact on industry than government, to get industry to understand that the elderly employee has a good work record, that he or she can be continued to be employed. Your thrust seems to be just to prepare people to retire, or help them after retirement.

Mr. Winick:

I don't believe the area you have identified is in fact seen as a high-priority matter by many unions. I don't know of any major effort to educate employers on the merits of hiring the older worker. There are a number of voluntary agencies with which the organized labor movement cooperates that do that, but I would say these agencies are not very potent.

Mr. Stieglitz:

In our local, when a person has grown old in the service, we give him an easier job. We place him somewhere where he will fit. That is written into our contract.

Mr. Winick:

There is another consideration when we talk about pressing government to assist the older worker. Government funds are more likely to go to help the younger person who is unemployed because of community concern about possible trouble, if unemployed young people are not given appropriate activity to drain off their energy or to focus their interest. Unfortunately for the older worker, I believe the younger generation is most likely to get primary attention from the legislators.

Ms. Litwak:

The City of New York very effectively gets rid of older workers by attrition. Contractually, it can't fire an older worker, it is illegal to do so. But you can put an older worker into a job that is just so miserable and demeaning, that you force that person to retire. So you are not firing that person, you just make working life unbearable. The City does this consistently. The City will stick with the younger employees, and knock the older ones out. To some degree they can get away with it. There is some collusion with the unions, it seems to me, because the unions also have to survive, and they are going to bank on the middle-aged and younger workers at this point. All of the older industrial cities that are unionized have exactly the same problem. You are not going to put your eggs in the basket of the older worker.

Audience:

The union is taking no more of an active stand than industry is, and both will have to be pushed by government.

Ms. Litwak:

I hate to say it, but that is fundamentally the way it is. However, there are exceptions, and I think unions can be educated and turned around.

Audience:

I do not understand why unions do not provide for reciprocity, so a person could make a transitional step to another job in another union. Unions do not encourage this kind of reciprocity. You are an electrical worker, and you are an electrical worker until you retire, and that is your problem. The unions themselves have not sought to help their brother and sister union members find transitional or circular careers so they can continue their life work cycle.

Mr. Winick:

A person can have any number of union cards, but the way unions have evolved, dividing up their turf with strong leaders carving out territory, lateral transfer is just not possible. However, many unions do make provisions, for those who wish to pursue alternate careers, to do so at union expense; this is one of the benefits that is negotiated. For example, I know a substantial number of people who, while working as electricians, decide that although they are paid pretty well, they would like to go to school to become social workers, or lawyers, or teachers. They remain in the electrical industry until they are sure they have a real commitment, and can get a job in another vocation. They are able to go to school at the expense of the union welfare fund because education is one of the benefits of their union membership.

Ms. Litwak:

In our college program, which is apart from our skills-upgrading classes, we have sequential programs built in, which make it possible for employees to leave City service if they want, and go into alternative careers. For instance, employees who graduate with a B.A. in social work can move to an entirely different job. Our tuition reimbursement system also makes it possible for a person to go on for a graduate degree with partial help from the union. We also have a part-time employment service which tries to place retired members. I would like to say that our rate of placement is very high, but it is not. That, I think, is not the union's problem, it is an economic problem. You are not going to get work if you are older; you certainly are going to be discriminated against. That can be said with certainty.

Audience:

We have talked a lot about the options that employees have as far as early retirement is concerned. Inasmuch as most people are guaranteed a job until they reach age 70, I am interested as a member of my union's health and welfare committee to try to provide appropriate services to the membership while they are working.

Mr. Stieglitz:

In our local, if a person retires at age 55, he will receive all medical provisions until he is age 65, at which time the benefit is coordinated with Medicare. Retirement at age 55 is based on age and years of service. A person with, say, 35 years of service can retire with 100 percent vestment at age 55. In that respect, we do take care of some of our people in the higher age bracket.

Audience:

As Mr. Bolch has pointed out, 70 can be a young age for retirement. Encouraging and allowing people to work beyond that age prevents retirement from being a problem and provides more funds for those who are working. The union's drive to develop good retirement programs, might, in effect, be part of the problem, as it makes retirement more attractive to people than continued employment.

Ms. Litwak:

I think unions are well aware of the fact that people have to work longer now. With double-digit inflation, a person may want to retire, but cannot. It seems to me you are saying, if the union didn't make retirement so attractive, if they cut out the benefits that have been negotiated for their members, if they didn't have programs and a variety of life-enhancing experiences available to them, the members would want to stay on and work. I submit to you that they want to stay on to work: but if they can't stay on to work, then the union has the responsibility to continue being concerned with them as human beings with needs after their retirement.

Audience:

I didn't mean to imply that the union should cut off benefits. What I am asking is, whether or not more energy should be directed toward interesting the employee in working as long as possible.

Mr. Stieglitz:

In our industry a mechanic who is subjected to all types of weather would not want to stay in that bailiwick when he gets on in years—whereas a mutuel clerk can stay on forever.

Audience:

I am an information and referral coordinator for senior citizens. We get calls all day long from people looking for tradespeople. They are looking to save a few dollars, so they are trying to find a retired person who needs supplementary income. Do any of the unions have part-time employment services for retired trades people?

Mr. Winick:

If you have a system of two rates of pay for the same work, you are creating a difficult situation for a union official to deal with. In other words, you are taking a $10 fee away from the functioning, active member so that a retired person can do the same work for $5. It would be an impossible situation if it were done on a formal, official basis. If an informal connection is made and you get a retired bricklayer to build a patio for you, just between you and him, that is one thing. But if you call the bricklayer's union and say you want them to recommend a retired bricklayer to work at a low rate, they will not cooperate.

Audience:

Are retirees involved in helping to bring about changes that could affect them, either through union management or through legislators?

Mr. Stieglitz:

Our union has a very active legislative committee and we have a perpetual lobby in Washington. Political action is the most effective method. We are trying to get the older people to become active in the lobby.

Ms. Litwak:

It is a two-step process. The first step is for the retirees themselves to get angry enough and assertive enough and visible enough to begin to turn the minds of the union leadership to their needs. That is what is happening in my union. It has taken about three years, but the first step was for the retirees just to be there, being pains in the neck. The essence of advocacy, the essence of political action, is to make a nuisance of yourself and do it single-mindedly. The retirees did that. The second step is to negotiate with the union leadership for certain prerogatives. The retirees made themselves heard, made noise, and the union began to mobilize its forces on their behalf.

Audience:

The elderly people we are dealing with were not brought up in a climate where we were supposed to be vocal. They need direction on how to go about it.

Mr. Stieglitz:

That is why I advocate pre-retirement seminars. They are very important. They stress that this type of attitude be developed, particularly the political aspect. I think you are going to hear more from the elderly in the future than ever before.

Audience:

When you speak of the elderly as a class, it is not really correct. The elderly person, just like any other person, has his own desires, his own wants, his own ideas. There really is no such thing as an elderly class with a common political motive. You'll find Republicans, Democrats, rich, poor, middle-class. You cannot really depend on a political movement of the elderly as such. The only thing that has been proven is that the elderly vote more often than any other group.

Mr. Stieglitz:

If you get them angry enough they'll vote as a group. When something is affecting them in the pocketbook, I can assure you they'll vote as a group.

Audience:

Yes, maybe on one particular issue, but by and large, they will not vote as a block. I see no reason why they should.

Ms. Litwak:

You are right. They are not a monolithic group, nor should they be viewed as one. But there are a number of reasons for them to unite on issues that affect their destinies and their lives.

REFERENCES

1 Siegmund H. May, M.D. *The Crowning Years.* New York: J.B. Lippincott Company, 1968, p. 13.

Chapter 4

A LOOK AT THE AGING EMPLOYEE —
MEDICAL ASPECTS

Morton Ward, M.D., F.A.C.P. *

Time has a way of changing things. The passage of time seems in some mysterious way to alter people, customs, life-styles, and even definitions. When 65 was the age of retirement, it was also the dividing line between the overripe adult and the elderly. The aging employee was then probably 60 years of age and considered to be approaching obsolescence. The age of mandatory retirement, except for special circumstances, is now 70 years of age. Has there been a corresponding change in the definition of the "aging employee"? We

*Dr. Ward received his medical degree in 1940 from Temple University. He served as Chief of Medicine at Frankford Hospital in Philadelphia, was a consultant in geriatric medicine at Hahnemann Medical College, and from 1964 to the present, Dr. Ward has been the Medical Director of the Philadelphia Geriatric Center.

Dr. Ward is a Fellow of the American College of Physicians, a Fellow of the American Geriatrics Society, and a Fellow of the Gerontological Society. He is President of the Pennsylvania Medical Directors Association, as well as Chairperson of the Committee on Aging of the Philadelphia County Medical Society.

Dr. Ward is Clinical Associate Professor of Medicine at Temple University and at the Medical College of Pennsylvania.

now understand the over-65 population much better, and speak of those from age 65 to 74 as the young aged, and those age 75 and older as the old aged. I feel that the 65-year-old of today is in general a much younger, more energetic and vibrant person than his counterpart of 30 years ago. I discovered a good deal of evidence supporting this a little over a year ago when I received an achievement award in the form of a red, white, and blue card from Medicare. It stated in invisible terms that I had the choice of lowering my standard of living or continuing to work. You have no idea, or do you, how young this can make you feel?

Most of my work in recent years dealt with those over age 65. As I gathered some health data so that I could better compare the 45 to 64 age group with those above 65, I noted that while I did not start smoking again, I began to take a drink a little oftener. One of the problems lies in attempting to define the transition point at which the relatively healthy 65-year-old becomes the relatively unhealthy over-65. Before presenting the statistics I should like to discuss some basic information related to the aging process.

There are many theories regarding the cause of aging. About 11 of these appear to have some substance. Whenever we have 11 or more theories, diagnoses, or treatments, you can be certain that none of them provides the complete answer. The conclusion is that we do not really understand the aging process. We know to a great extent *what* happens, but we do not understand the *why*, or the mechanism.

What happens is very evident to even a casual observer. The appearance changes, the skin becomes yellowed, somewhat flaccid and inelastic. Wrinkles and lines appear as well as an increase in pigmented, keratotic, and telangiectatic lesions. Cartilage becomes calcified and the skeleton decalcified. Degenerative changes increase in the joints and may cause pain or limitation in mobility. The brittle bones fracture with less trauma, and hip fractures are for the most part a malady of the elderly. The vertebrae tend to become compressed and even wedged, so that by age 80 there tends to be a one-inch decrease in height, and a tendency toward kyphosis or hunchback. Skeletal muscle is decreased in volume and replaced by fat and connective tissue. There is an increase in the rigidity of the fibrous tissue and a progressive loss of elasticity of the arterial wall. The mineral content of the vessel wall, especially calcium, increases. Function of blood-forming organs remains intact.

The digestive system undergoes many changes. Nutrition may suffer as a result of loss of teeth or ill-fitting dentures. Hiatal hernia increases in incidence with age as does diverticula in the colon. The secretion of hydrochloric acid in the stomach is decreased, but generally digestion and absorption are unimpaired. By age 80 about half of the functioning kidney units are gone. So long as no problems stressing the kidney occur, the aged kidney manages but has decreased reserve capacity. Prostatic hypertrophy increases with age and may require surgical intervention. While the reproductive system of the male continues to function into old age, the capacity for reproduction and cessation of menstruation usually occurs between ages 45 and 50 in the female. Menopause may run the entire scale in severity of symptoms for the female, but existence of a male climacteric is still controversial. Thyroid function tends to decrease with age and tolerance for glucose also diminishes. Adrenal function changes little.

Some of the most distressing symptoms are related to decrease or loss of effective function in the special sense organs and the nervous system. Visual impairment or loss due to cataracts, glaucoma, macular degeneration, or retinal detachments can alter the capability to cope with one's needs in relation to the environment. Some blindness is preventable and some at present is untreatable. Loss of hearing, especially in the higher frequencies, may impair communication and enjoyment of certain forms of entertainment.

Nervous-system changes may result in intellectual, memory, and orientation deficits. Senile dementia and Parkinsonism are two of the major nervous system afflictions of the elderly. The boundary between the organic (neurological) and functional (psychiatric) disease is becoming less distinct as our knowledge increases. Brain function and behavior remain as frontiers in medicine requiring extensive exploration.

I do not wish to give the impression that aging inevitably brings with it "second childhood" and marked impairment of mental function. Most elderly remain mentally intact into advanced age. I am reminded of an actual incident at our Center a number of years ago when one of our residents approaching 104 years of age was engaged in a heated discussion with his daughter who was about 78 years of age. He was complaining bitterly about persistent pain in his left foot which the doctors were unable completely to relieve. His daughter tried to console him, stating, "Pop, you have to realize and accept such things as you grow older." His curt but appropriate reply was, "Don't tell me such nonsense. My right foot is just as old as my left, and it doesn't hurt."

I have tried to give a superficial overview of some of the anatomic and physiological changes that accompany the aging process. The distinction as to which changes are the result of disease and which are part of so-called "normal aging" remains to be clarified. Judgments are difficult when the underlying processes are ill-defined.

Much of the health information that has been gathered is classified in certain categories with respect to age. For our purposes, we are mainly interested in data for 45-64 years and over 65 years. When available we prefer to see the over-65 group divided into 65 to 74 years and those over 75 years. With the advent of Medicare we are now getting much better information regarding the over-65 group.

Aging persons become more vulnerable to health problems, although most will remain relatively well and functional for many years. Let's look at some of these facts.

A vital and health statistics report estimated that in June 1978 there were 212,989,000 people in the United States, and of these 43,382,000 (20.3 percent) were between 45 and 64 years of age. Those 65 years and over totaled 22,528,000 or 10.5 percent. There were twice as many persons employed between ages 17 and 44 as compared to those 45 years and over. The incidence of acute conditions (illness and injury combined) per 100 persons per year declined as age increased. However, the number of days of restricted activity due to acute conditions increased progressively with age—4.3 days in the 17-44 year group, 6.1 days in the 45-64 group, and 10.9 in the 65 and over group. With respect to bed disability due to acute conditions, the duration in days for the same groups are 1.9, 2.5, and 4.6 days respectively.

The conclusion would appear to be that you have less chance of becoming acutely ill or injured as you grow older, but your tolerance of such events will decrease and you will spend more days at home and/or in bed than your younger counterpart. The above statistics cover infectious disease, respiratory, and gastrointestinal conditions and injuries of all types. I saw no information relating to the relative rates of complete recovery, residual disability (chronic disease), and partial or total disability resulting from these acute conditions. It seems obvious, however, that the impact of acute illness or injury increases in severity with age. Despite this, it is interesting to note that regarding days lost from work per 100 currently employed persons per year, those 45 years and over lost fewer days than those 17 to 44 years of age.

The proportion of persons hospitalized varies with age, with a higher percentage of people 65 years and over than those in younger age groups. Also, older persons were more likely than younger ones to have had three or more episodes in a single year. Increasing age paralleled an increasing average number of days spent in the hospital and total days of hospitalization during the reference period (1972). The percentage hospitalized was essentially the same for the 15 to 44 and 45 to 64 age groups but jumped almost 5 percent for those 65 years and over. The hospital stay however went from 7.2 days (15-44 years), to 13.1 days (45-64 years) and to 17.5 days for those 65 years and over.

When we consider the percent distribution of persons with limitation of activity due to chronic conditions, we find some very disturbing facts. The percentage of persons with activity limitation almost triples from the 17 to 44 age group to the 45 to 64 age group, and almost doubles again between the latter and the 65-and-over age group. The same proportions hold for limitation in a major activity, while 76.4 percent of those 45-64 years of age have no activity limitation, this drops to 55 percent for those age 65 and over. Whether causing disability or activity limitation or not, 80 percent of those over age 65 suffer from one or more chronic diseases.

As one advances in age, so usually does one also advance in his vocation, and increased income brings with it more responsibility and greater stress both at work and at home. Raising and educating a family can bring both emotional and economic turmoil—especially when a gifted child decides to major in Mesopotamian anthropology. Employees are bombarded on all sides by announcements of courses and seminars, and the necessity to attend by direct order or by feelings of insecurity that failure to attend may be misinterpreted—when what we really need is a vacation.

And what is the nature of the onslaught? How to manage by delegating management to those less able to manage, how to minimize stress when production falls while you attended seminars, how to quit your job and make more money giving seminars to those who will lose their jobs because of attending your conferences. If you have a "Type A" behavior pattern you will be a success but you will also have a "coronary." Solution: change to a "Type B" personality. You might become a failure but at least you can die of something else, like cancer.

Forgive me if I appear to be frivolous with such a serious subject. What I am really trying to do is make an appeal to a rare trait—common sense. It is equally undesirable to lack concern and invite disaster by flouting all rules of health as to be so concerned as to become depressed and neurotic. Live moderately and sensibly but live today, now. Do not exist for tomorrow alone, tomorrow may not be what you planned for.

To maintain mental as well as physical well-being, coping with today and hoping for a better tomorrow is insufficient. We need to feel that "now" is just as meaningful as the future "then," and act and plan accordingly. There is increasing evidence that the old adage about a healthy mind in a healthy body is more than just a turn of phrase. Since the discovery of hormonal releasing factors in the hypothalamus of the brain and nerve pathways between the hypothalamus and the higher centers, the effect of the psyche on the soma is becoming clearer. There are psychological studies that indicate an increased susceptibility to cancer in certain emotional states. Recent knowledge about internal mechanisms for control of pain by the release of certain substances, called endorphins, by the brain, have led to theories regarding its control by mental processes such as suggestion and by physical means such as acupuncture. But let's leave the realm of mental health, since this has been and I am sure will be addressed further during this meeting.

You have been given to this point the bad news about aging, and I will sum up the morose part of my dissertation by the following unhappy advice. The triumverate of a miserable senescence is aging, sickness, and poverty. The essence of tragedy is to get old, sick, and poor at the same time.

If the statistics regarding health and aging are rather dismal, there are hopeful signs that progress in medicine may facilitate earlier diagnosis and more effective therapy in the future. There are also indications, for reasons that are not clear, that two of the three major diseases associated with aging are declining in incidence; namely acute myocardial infarction and stroke. Progress seems slow, but gains are being made against the other member of the trio, cancer.

A recent major breakthrough rivalling the discovery of penicillin in importance, has been the invention of computerized tomography. This permits sectional visualization of the brain and body and allows us to see areas previously hidden from view. We have every expectation that refinement of present methods and the advent of new ones as well as new and more specific medications will impede the advance of age-related decrements in function. The main problem is to avoid loss of function.

Now to the brighter side. At some point along the continuum of life, responsibilities toward others diminish and it is to be hoped that obligation to self becomes the preponderant theme for the remainder of life. Most young aged are still functioning at higher than adequate levels and there is much to be said for early retirement. But only if you are prepared to enjoy it—to revel in the freedom from the constraints of daily routine and the luxury of time as a servant instead of a master. One should develop expertise in avocations early in life. It may be difficult for a "retiree" to learn a new skill or hobby. The "know-how" should already be in place, ready to be enjoyed, without the frustrations which are poorly tolerated in the later years. To be prepared for a "successful" old age, one requires good health and proper planning. Good health cannot be guaranteed, but there are many things that can be done to minimize the ravages of time. One can avoid excesses in all forms—alcohol, tobacco, and overwork without proper rest or relaxation. You may find that productivity is not necessarily a function of time and creativity is difficult under the duress of fatigue. Playing too hard is just as bad as working too hard. Good physical condition is essential to a feeling of well being. However, the body of a 60-plus person is not really capable of the physical performance of a youth of 20.

There are rare exceptions in which physical conditioning has been an ongoing rather than a sporadic way of life. Lee Trevino recently commented on his professional golfing career: "It's coming to an end. I don't hit it as close to the flag as I used to. I don't putt like I used to. Hell, when you get old, you don't do anything like you used to.'' How old was he when he said this? He was 40. Old is relative: relative to the task you are performing, relative to what others expect of you, but most important, relative to what you expect of yourself. Why must we forever compete? There comes a time as our values and our aspirations change, that the quarry is no longer worth the chase. But time can be an enemy to a retired person unprepared to cope effectively with it. Unfortunately there are many persons to whom work constitutes the entirety of their existence, and when the daily routine of going to work ends, a void results that cannot be filled. Being prepared, therefore, means also planning for a full, satisfying career of activities you always wanted to take up but didn't have the time. But let these be compatible with your physical, mental, and emotional attributes.

There are many ways in which an older individual can maximize what he has rather than dwell on what he has lost or never had at all. There is little reason to arrive at retirement sans teeth, sans vision and sans hearing. Many of these deficits are preventable or correctable if proper care is exercised. Every complaint, every problem has a cause; the earlier help is sought, the earlier the diagnosis is made, the more effective is treatment, as a general rule. The list of what is now available and what we see forthcoming portends a longer meaningful and productive life for the aging employee. The concept of good health is a holistic one encompassing physical, mental, social, and emotional well-being. A person is more than the sum total of his or her parts and is capable of enjoying life to the fullest only when achieving the inner contentment that comes from a positive approach in making the most of what one has, rather than dwelling on what one has not. Regardless of age, live in the present—while you prepare for the future. To quote John Greenleaf Whittier: ''For of all sad words of tongue or pen, the saddest are these: 'It might have been.' ''

If I am permitted to change a few words in the poem by Robert Herrick written in 1648, the title would become, ''To Aging Employees to Make Much of Time.'' The verses, as changed, seem very appropriate in closing:

> Gather ye rosebuds while ye may:
>   Old Time is still a-flying;
> And this same flower that smiles today,
>   Tomorrow will be dying.

The glorious lamp of heaven, the sun,
    The higher he's a-getting
The sooner will his race be run,
    And nearer he's to setting.

That age is best which is the first,
    When youth and blood are warmer;
But being spent, the worse, and worst
    Times still succeed the former.

Then be not coy, but use your time;
    And while ye may, be merry;
For having lost but once your prime,
    You'll not forever tarry.

DISCUSSION

Discussants on this panel, chaired by Dr. Morton Ward, were: Jerome L. Blaunstein, M.D., Medical Director, New York City Region, A.T. & T. Long Lines; Penny W. Budoff, M.D., Assistant Professor of Clinical Family Medicine, School of Medicine, Health Sciences Center, State University of New York at Stony Brook; Frances Dowdy, R.N., Director of Nursing, Broadlawn Manor Nursing Home & Health-Related Facility; and Julian H. Schwartz, M.D., a private practitioner in Internal Medicine and Gastroenterology, and a consultant to South Oaks Hospital.

Ms. Dowdy:

It has been well stated at this conference that there exists a pressing need to find ways to provide better, more efficient health care for older Americans. As a nation we are steadily growing older. By the end of this century some 32 million people of our nation, one-eighth of our total population, will be 65 or older. The objective is not merely to extend the years of life but to improve the quality of life in one's later years. As Dr. Robert N. Butler, Director of theNational Institute of Aging, has emphasized, our challenge is to extend the fruitful middle years, healthy and vigorous years, in which we can live creatively to the best of our ability, carrying our own weight and paying our own way as productive contributors to society, thereby hanging on to our independence and self-direction.

Management has become aware of the increasing need for health care benefits for employees. With the institution of these benefits we have partially recognized the increasing needs of the aging employee. But, does our responsibility end with these provisions? I believe not. Now that the retirement age has been extended to age 70, management more than ever will be called upon to meet health care needs and to help employees solve their health problems in these later years of employment. Managers will have to become more aware that with age comes the start of various chronic diseases—heart disease, anemia, alcoholism, hypertension, cataracts, mental depression, to mention only some of the major ones. Management must be cognizant that if any employee who is struggling with the knowledge of a newly-diagnosed chronic illness is properly counseled and supported through this stress period, he can be maintained as a productive, functioning employee. The alternative will be to relegate the employee to the scrap heap, which instead of solving his problem will only create more.

Everyone at the management level will have to be sensitive to an employee whose work performance is not up to expectation, and try to get this employee into our newly-created services for prompt relief of his problem. Our health care services will have to include counseling services for those with emotional or social problems; screening services to pick up the hypertensive, the early diabetic, the anemic, etc.; education services to teach our employees how to live productively with a chronic ailment. Thought must be put into programs to help the aging employee plan better for the retirement years. This must not wait till the employee announces a retirement date. Workers must start finding a second career or interest earlier, probably not later than their early 50's. Industry must realize that the older we become, the more unique as individuals we become. With increasing age each person is more uniquely expressive of the interplay between hereditary characteristics and environment. Older men and women cannot be regarded as a homogenous group. Industry will be challenged more than ever to cooperate with existing community services and to help create new ones to meet the needs of their older, but still valuable, employees.

Dr. Budoff:

From my vantage point I think that a change in mental attitude will come slowly but surely in this country. We are now very much a youth-oriented nation, but this orientation will change if only because of the ever-increasing numbers of older citizens. We are beginning to see some of these changes today. All of a sudden it is not so bad to be 40. Many of the famous female movie stars are 40 and, what is more, they are admitting it, even flaunting it. As for industry, the employer sets the tone in his factory or his office. All too often his attitude has been negative toward the aging employee. Frequently, the plan is simply to make the older employee so uncomfortable that he will leave. But as the baby-boom legacy ends, and fewer younger, less expensive workers are coming into the work force, the older employee will become extremely valuable.

There is a difference between how men and women age. We all know that women live longer than men. I have wondered why that is, and have concluded that women are really much better rounded—in several ways. I think our personalities are better rounded; we haven't been channeled so narrowly. Men have been trained to be men, to go to work, come home and be taken care of. But women have been trained to grow up and take care of their men and take care of themselves and their children and do the washing and ironing, and in today's economy most women have to go back to work as well. Somehow women are able to function at the factory and at home at the same time.

This is important, for as they get older and leave work it's not the only thing they have in their life. Indeed, women may still have their kids to take care of. They still have dinner to cook. They still have household errands and other chores to aggravate them. I think that is why women do better. We have more things to drive us crazy, and these keep us on an even keel through all our years. We are more in touch with the basic processes of life. Women are more social than men, and often have several close friendships with other women. When men get to be 65, they are suddenly looking at an empty life ahead of them. All of a sudden they have to go out and learn: learn to relax, to make social friends, learn how to fish. They have to find something to do. They are not accustomed to that. They know little else but work to fill their days. But there are changes coming. We are finally getting across to men that they don't have to be "masculine" all the time. They can wash dishes, or change the baby's diaper, or cook a meal. Men who can take part in these daily tasks will have more to round out their lives as they get older. There will be more to life than just the job from eight to five.

Dr. Blaunstein:

By the year 2030, we are going to see a jump from 31 million to 52 million people over the age of 65. Society will have to cope with that number of people, and industry will have to extend itself in order to provide meaningful employment for the number of elderly people who will be available as valuable employees.

For long periods of time industry will derive the maximum benefit from the skills which employees have developed over the years. It must also be pointed out that there is a moral and ethical obligation to keep the elderly person employed so that he is self-sufficient. Industry owes it to valued employees to do just that. I would also like to point out that women, for the reasons that Dr. Budoff pointed out, live longer.

My point of view is perhaps just a shade less feminist than medical. Women have a higher level of high-density lipoprotein which keeps them in a way protected from coronary artery disease. It is a well known fact that men are more prone to coronaries. That is one factor. On a more optimistic note, I think that, medically speaking, and on the basis of my relatively brief medical career of 27 years, medicine has contributed very substantially to the maintenance of good health. Anesthetics and surgical procedures have been designed and geared specifically for the elderly, so that the mortality and morbidity associated with their illnesses are considerably reduced. A person can now sustain a hip fracture, for example, which is one of the afflications of elderly, and be restored very quickly so as to be able to function and even to work while the fracture is healing. We no longer put people in traction for hip fractures; we pin them and restore them quickly. We don't put wrist fractures in a cast so the person will get a stiff wrist. We can put in a small pin, and again, restore them quickly. That is the optimistic note. I think we have made great contributions along those lines.

Dr. Ward:

Something disturbs me a little bit. We are constantly talking about work, work, work. We have got to get them jobs, we have got to keep them in jobs. If they lose one job, we have to get them another job. Tell me, what is so bad about goofing off? You know, maybe you are entitled. What is this work ethic that you have got to work? I think I am getting to a point where I'd just as soon not work, if I can get away with it. Now the question is, how do you get away with it? How do you get away with it in a way which makes that kind of a life appealing? Why do I have to work to the day before I die?

Audience:

You need the money to retire and pursue other activities, happy activities. We are all looking forward to that. Nobody wants to work to the day before he dies.

Dr. Budoff:

Maybe there ought to be jobs created where you can work on a Monday only. Wouldn't that be nice? A little extra pocket money and you have the rest of the week off. Or work Monday and Wednesday. On the other hand, I just advised a man who has some health problems to retire at 62. Not everybody is the same, and I don't think we can treat everybody as if they were all made out of one mold. Some people do want to retire early, some people want to retire at 65 or later. No one is saying you to work. I don't think I want to work until I am 70. On the other hand, if I wanted to do something, I wouldn't be happy to be told I couldn't because I was past 65.

Dr. Blaunstein:

My remarks previously addressed those people who really wanted to work past the age of mandatory retirement, not in any way implying that everybody would wish to do so. Industry should, on the other hand, assist the employee in planning a retirement in such a way that it would be the most beneficial. I think we should see to health needs before they retire and instruct them in retirement planning as well as in health care. That is a part of industrial responsibility for the employee.

Ms. Dowdy:

I think we have to recognize that we are a work-oriented society. It has been ingrained in us from childhood, and I believe we are doing the same thing to our children today. Work comes before play. Mother does it to her son, to her daughter. Can I go out to play? Yes, clean your room first, take care of all your chores first. Work before play. We are at the other end of the spectrum in our jobs right now, working in a nursing home, and we find a great need to teach these older people how to play without guilt.

Audience:

You are not going to have people able to retire comfortably and play if the government reduces Social Security payments and ties them into one lump sum with a pension plan, as the government is planning to do. I'd love to retire and have a big pension, but if our government says let's limit the amount of pension and Social Security, I can't stop working and start playing.

Audience:

We are talking about retiring, but what about the employee who sees himself aging but still has a service to render? We must help retain the valuable employee regardless of age, and we must help the others accept retirement and point them in the right direction so a transition can be made with the least possible amount of psychic trauma.

Dr. Blaunstein:

It seems to me that your comment is in two parts. The first part deals with the active employee who has an emotional problem that impacts on his work performance. My region has an employee counselor. He is not a psychiatrist, but he is a professional who will evaluate the problem. He is equipped further to refer that particular employee to the proper authority for treatment, whether it be psychiatric, whether it be alcoholism, drugs, or whether family counseling is needed. This is for the active and valued employee, a trained person whom the company wants to hold for obvious reasons, having invested time and a great deal of money. Morally, we owe our employees this. It is part and parcel of our medical department's service.

The second part of your question has to do with pre-retirement planning. The moment a person in our company becomes eligible for retirement, which could be many years before it actually takes place, we have a seminar and we go over it completely. How much is taken out of their salaries toward retirement, and how much is set aside? The Social Security, and even the medical aspects are gone over. We sit there in panel so that all the employees who are eligible for retirement can ask pertinent questions. They can also meet with us privately in the medical department to go over their particular medical needs.

Audience:

I have been involved in the telephone industry for close to 40 years now, and I have seen tremendous technological changes occur. The equipment that we are now installing is displacing a great number of employees. More and more of the equipment is becoming automated, and many employees are being replaced by this automated equipment. They are very concerned about the loss of jobs. It has been coming for years, the last 25 years, but now it is approaching at a more rapid rate. My question is, from a medical point of view, have you seen any adverse effect on aging employees because of these technological advances and this displacement?

Dr. Blaunstein:

I think the Bell System, traditionally, has made great efforts to see that employees are not displaced because of technological advances. What we do see, however, from a medical point of view, is anxiety generated by fear of the unknown.

Dr. Budoff:

I would like to discuss the preparation for getting older and the preparation for retirement. That preparation, as far as I am concerned, begins today. You have been you a long time. Whether you are 62, or 64 doesn't make one iota of difference. Your personality traits have been there for a long time and the only thing I am really ever aware of is that as people get older their personalities intensify. The people who can't cope at 20 can't cope at 40, and surely can't cope at 65. So you had better get some help and learn to cope now, because it gets harder as you grow older.

Audience:

One observation I've made bothers me more as I get older. I see, and hear of, people who are planning for their retirement, seem to be looking forward to it, who retire and then become seriously ill or die. One of my theories is that perhaps this happens because of the abrupt change of rhythm in this person's life. I wonder if there is anything medically to be said that would indicate a kind of weaning away from work rather than simply stopping.

Dr. Schwartz:

Yes, what you say is very true. There are the beginnings now of some medical knowledge in the area of sudden-death syndrome which would tie into this. Many instances have been recorded of sudden death due to a cardiac arrhythmia, and this would occur in people not while they were stressed, but after the removal of the stress. We do not fully understand why; but it has something to do with a rearrangement of the autonomic nervous system which sometimes goes through a phase and has not adjusted into the relaxation phase. In this in-between phase, people have been known to develop various cardiac problems. Certainly a person who has been under a lot of pressure on a job, and suddenly was retired with nothing to do, would go through a period where he would be at high risk. After an interval, this risk would start to diminish. There are probably many other mechanisms that we don't understand which relate to this. We often see people who shortly after retirement, become severely disabled and have to spend the rest of their days in a nursing home.

Dr. Budoff:

Yes, you have to realize that after he leaves that high-stress job, he is still under tremendous mental stress. This new stress is created by the loss of a well-known daily routine and a feeling of suddenly being in limbo.

Dr. Schwartz:

Also, retirement itself is a major stress. He may not have a medical catastrophe immediately upon retirement as he is still going through the stress of adjusting to retirement, but once that is over there may be a vulnerable period.

Dr. Budoff:

Again, there are many, many things that have to be coped with along life's highway. Retirement is one of them. Losing a spouse is another. There are many things that happen. Some people cope better than others. I saw a woman this morning in my office who was terribly upset. I asked what the matter was. "Well," she said, "I bought a new rug and they delivered it in the wrong shade." Can you imagine what will happen to her when something *serious* goes wrong? Some things are important and some are not. You have to let unimportant things roll off your back. Again it is often your own personality that will do you in. And, as the years go by, if you fail to mend your personality flaws, they will get worse and worse, as any psychiatrist who is sitting here will tell you.

Dr. Blaunstein:

I think planning is the key word. If you plan your retirement well in advance, I think you can cope with it far more successfully than if you retired unplanned. You have got to retire to something.

You have got to be financially secure, you have to retire in good health, you have to have plans for pleasure and for activity and family. It has all got to be laid out for you so that you retire not *from*, but *to* something.

Dr. Ward:

There is something I want to throw back to the audience. You say you can't cope at 20, you can't cope at 40, you can't cope at 60. How do we get the person who can't cope at 40 to be able to cope at 60?

Dr. Budoff:

I think the question is, how do we get people to feel alive? How do we get people to be interested in life, to wake up in the morning and feel good and say, I want to get out of bed today, I want to see things, I want to do things. How do we do that?

Audience:

In many of the young men I see in my private practice the aging process has already started. We must also consider emotional age. Dr. Budoff, self-image is what makes you feel you want to get up in the morning; not what you are going to *do*, but what it *means* to you. If industry can find the proper channel for its employees of any age, I think it would give them self-esteem and a lot of the problems would disappear. In dealing with men whose self-esteem is low, I run psychological tests and if they have a high I.Q., I use what I call asset therapy. If they have had difficulty in their work, in their company, I say, forget about your neurosis, forget about your difficulties, you are on the ball, take advantage of it! Go back and take courses. Do this, do that. What we must do is raise their self-esteem. I think industry understands pretty well how to do that.

Dr. Budoff:

I don't know that industry knows how to do that.

Audience:

I think any measure of a successful manager is getting the people to do the job and enjoy doing the job. I have 20 supervisors reporting to me who have about 125 people under them. I would say that 65 percent of our work force are 55 years or older, and this is a production job. The supervisors have risen up from the ranks, have grown up with these people. They know them. They know their families. I have found in my experience that the measure of a successful supervisor is his ability to get that guy to do his job. With that, come all aspects of dealing with a person.

Dr. Budoff:

If every person here were like you, we wouldn't be having a conference.

Dr. Schwartz:

This may all be true, and in certain industries I am sure it is done well. But looking at it from my point of view, as a private-practice physician, seeing the people come into my office, there are an awful lot of older people who are unhappy with their jobs. They really don't have much self-esteem and are just biding their time, just waiting to retire. If they could find some way to get out on disability they would love to.

Audience:

We are hearing, what are *we* going to do for people who are getting ready to retire? My question is, what are *they* doing for themselves? We can provide anybody with the tools to do something, but will they use them and do something for themselves? In our society today, how much do we have to give people in order for them to respond? Our culture is a great big giveaway.

Dr. Budoff:

I don't think anybody wants something for nothing.

Dr. Ward:

We have gotten to the point where we ask: What does industry expect from me as an employee? What do others expect of me as a member of a family or a community? What do I expect of myself? How about the question of the medical situation and expectations of aging employees? What are reasonable expectations? What do you think you are entitled to? How much should be given to you? How much should you do for yourself? You see, government is already saying, hey, this is costing too much.

Dr. Schwartz:

I have years ahead of me before I retire, but one thing I am expecting—not expecting but hoping—is that at least I will have my health. I think that is what everybody looks forward to with hope.

Dr. Blaunstein:

Dr. Ward, you said it yourself, to be old, to be sick, and to be poor is pretty bad. People expect to be old, you can't help that; but not to be poor and not be sick.

Dr. Ward:

And don't be both at the same time. Let's narrow it down a little bit. What do you expect, as you get older, to receive in the way of protection against catastrophic illness that could wipe out everything you worked for all your life? What do you expect the government to do? What do you expect your employer to do? What do you expect to do for yourselves? These are the questions we are going to be addressing more and more in the immediate future.

Audience:

In this country we wait until we are ill and then we want a miracle; whereas if we had learned earlier in life to live a healthier life we would have less problems. Government and industry should be putting their emphasis with employees on prevention and education.

Dr. Ward:

Whose responsibility? Somebody has got to be responsible.

Dr. Blaunstein:

I think the person himself has got to do it. You can throw a lot of educational theories at people, but it is their ultimate responsibility to care for their bodies and minds, the total person. Of course, if you live a good life while you are young, get into the habit of proper exercise, proper diet, attention to whatever illness you may have, I think you are going to live longer and better. But the responsibility is the individual's.

Dr. Ward:

What are reasonable expectations from either your Federal government or your state government or your employer? What is reasonable to expect, because everything you see now is based on cost-consciousness and cost-control.

Dr. Budoff:

Of course many corporations do have employee health programs. They give physicals, Pap smears, breast examinations: they do all kinds of things within the company. This country places tremendous emphasis on medical facts and medical fiction. The media bombard us daily. You can't turn on the news without hearing about some new discovery, or how you should have this or that examination or test. Pick up any magazine or newspaper, and you will find a health column. If you really want to, you can read yourself into the ground; there are lots of health books on hypertension, dieting, health—you name it.

There is also increasing emphasis on health education. Blue Shield and Blue Cross are starting a program to educate people. There are other groups that give lectures for a fee that will teach you about your own health; taking your own blood pressure, knowing when you really have to go to the doctor. Self-care is becoming much more a part of life. People are starting to take more responsibility for their own bodies. The concern with health and medicine is good because most people are not knowledgeable about their own bodies. I see many women in my practice—lawyers, engineers, accountants, social workers—and when I ask them about their medical history, they don't know why any procedure was undertaken, and these are educated women. More and more patients are becoming assertive, and doctors are going to have to get sharper because their patients are getting wiser.

Audience:

I'm a nurse. We have to have a yearly physical, and over age 50, a cardiogram. I have a history of hypertension which I tend to ignore because I don't have symptoms. Changes were noticed in my last cardiogram, so I immediately went to see my own doctor. I was put on medication and I never lost a day's work. I feel great. But if I didn't have that yearly physical and if I wasn't pressed into having the cardiogram, I don't know where I'd be.

Dr. Blaunstein:

What you are describing is preventive medicine. You don't want to wait until you get symptoms of high blood pressure, you want to treat it well before that.

We have come full circle here. These are the things that people should do for themselves to reach a successful old age. Treat your body well in advance and do it right—keep the weight down, stop smoking, watch your blood pressure, and so on. Industry can help to do that by providing check-ups in the industrial setting. Blood-pressure checks can be done in every medical department for thousands of employees with no problem whatsoever and many will turn up unsuspected and then be treated. That would be a great contribution on the part of industry.

Dr. Ward:

Of course, the medical profession does not say to the employee, we have all the answers. We are trying to advise you the best way we know how. How do we get the cooperation of the employee? How do we maximize the use of information we already have, so that the employee will have a chance to survive to the point where we can hope to change retirement so that it becomes a part of a successful life rather than a dismal failure at the end of the tunnel? As you are getting older, what do you expect in the way of medical care? Is the sky the limit? What is reasonable? You who are in the health professions know the constraints that are being put on what is reasonable.

Audience:

What about an employee who, as he gets older, just can't do his job as well?

Dr. Schwartz:

It is unfortunate, but the world is a rough place and when people can't do their jobs they just can't be carried. If a baseball player can no longer hit, he loses his job. If I could no longer function in my present capacity, I would have to do something else or retire early. I am not just going to be protected. The same standard should apply to a teacher who could no longer teach effectively or, for that matter, to any jobholder.

All of this is unfortunate, it is sad, but I don't feel that people should just be carried along when they reach the point that they no longer can do their jobs. If possible, they should be transferred to another position where they could still function adequately. This is very difficult for many people to accept. I don't feel that industry has a responsibility to carry people in positions they cannot effectively fill.

Dr. Ward:

What we are talking about is the need of a corporation or whatever it is, to be productive, to be efficient, and, on the other hand, also minimize the stress related to job and security of individuals working for them. How paternal shall the company become? Again, what are reasonable expectations?

Audience:

I think we have made a lot of advances in industry in humanizing the whole job.

Dr. Budoff:

Yes. Businesses, especially bigger corporations, can train people in supervisory positions to recognize and alleviate the stress on their subordinates.

Audience:

The question was asked, what do we expect in terms of medical help? I am talking from the standpoint of a large corporation, and I think that our health plan is a pretty good one for retirees. The coverage they get after they retire is almost the same as they had when they were working.

Dr. Schwartz:

Right now Medicare takes care of most of the medical costs for people 65 and over. However, a big problem for retired people is that Medicare does not cover the cost of drugs. I can very easily prescribe seven or eight different medicines that my elderly patients really need, but when they have to buy these medications on an ongoing basis month after month, this gets to be a very big burden.

In general, most of the medical care, after 65, is already covered. Catastrophic care is something that, I think, is really the next step. I think that organized medicine itself certainly supports a catastrophic type of medical care. I think that this probably will be the next thing to be instituted in this country for people of all ages. It really shouldn't cost that much. It is enormously expensive for an individual if he were to have a catastrophic illness, but it doesn't occur so frequently that the cost to the country would be that much. The country can well afford that. As for other more costly medical plans to be paid for by the government, we must remember that these costs ultimately fall back on the people. The government doesn't really pay for anything. We pay. We will have to pay the government, and industry will have to pay the government, in the form of taxes to cover all of these costs. So it really becomes a question of just how we are going to spread the cost around. I think most working people today do have some form of insurance. But there are many people who are not working, and these are the people who often don't have insurance. These are problems that have to be worked out. And, no matter what my personal feelings are, I don't think that we are about to have socialized medicine in the near future. As much as the politicians like to talk about it, I don't think anybody is ready to pay for anything like that. I don't think this country can afford it.

Audience:

If the government is going to pay for everyone from the cradle to the grave, we are all going to pick it up.

Dr. Ward:

Neither the government nor industry nor anything can be all things to all people. What we are still trying to answer is, is the aging employee looking to government, looking to industry, and saying, I'm getting older, what happens to me if I get sick? This is the question we are trying to address. How far does it go? Where does it stop? Where's your responsibility vis-a-vis somebody else's responsibility? How much do you expect me to pay for your illness? On the other hand, there's the aging employee saying, if I take good care of myself, nothing is going to happen to me. But as you get older, catastrophic illness is unpredictable. You are fine today, and you may have a stroke tomorrow. So, we are just touching on the subject. We have a long way to go.

Chapter 5

OLD AGE, EMPLOYMENT, AND SOCIAL NETWORK

Rose Laub Coser, Ph.D.*

'tis our fast intent
To shake all cares and business from our age;
Conferring them on younger strengths, while we
Unburden'd crawl toward death.''

King Lear

It has been said that retirement is peculiar to industrial society, that there is no problem of "retirement" in rural or other pre-industrial society. So stated, this is a myth. In some rural societies provi-

*Rose Laub Coser, Ph.D., is Professor of Community and Preventive Medicine at the Health Sciences Center and Professor of Sociology in the Department of Sociology at the State University of New York at Stony Brook. She has written on general hospitals (*Life in the Ward*, East Lansing, Michigan State University Press, 1962) and mental hospitals (*Training in Ambiguity: Learning Through Doing in a Mental Hospital*, New York: The Free Press, 1979), on the social structure of the family (*The Family, Its Structure and Functions*, Thoroughly Revised Edition with new Introduction, New York: St. Martin's, 1974), and on the theory of social structure. She has been a Fellow at Clare Hall in Cambridge, England (1975-76), and at the Center for Advanced Study in the Behavioral Sciences at Stanford, Ca. (1979-80), and has held a Guggenheim fellowship also in 1979-80. At present she is doing research on the social roles of immigrant women.

129

sions may exist for older people to relinquish or sharply decrease their productive activities—as the example of the old Irish couple retiring to the West Room upon the marriage of a son testifies.[1] As Jack Goody has pointed out, "The decreasing powers of the aged, at least in the economic sphere, lead inevitably to a reduction of their role in the fields, the pastures, or the woods [and] the formal transfer of these resources weakens their control over the junior generation, with the possible result of neglect or nonsupport."[2]

Yet it would be closer to the truth to say that in non-industrial societies there is no fixed age when this takes place. There is likely to be no residential separation between the place of work one withdraws from—entirely or in part—and the home. Old age marks the passing on, or the anticipation of passing on, of family resources and family values to the next generation. So-called retirement in such societies is linked to kin relationships.

Also, in industrial societies, more people are living to be old. A higher proportion of any birth cohort is living to be older than the previous cohort. In 1905, in the U.S., the odds for white males born that year reaching the age of 65 was roughly 66 out of 100, in contrast to only 53 out of 100 for those born 40 years earlier in 1865 (the year 1865 is frequently cited as the launching of the Industrial Age in the United States.) At the same time, however, workers increasingly have retired before age sixty-five.[3] The ranks of the retired have been swelling irrespective of longevity and the birth rate, because it has been possible to do with proportionately fewer people who produce goods and services.

The participation of men aged 65 to 69 in the work force has steadily declined. In 1950, approximately 60 percent of males in this age group in the U.S. were in the labor force. But by 1970, the proportion declined to 41 percent. What is more, this proportion includes, to a greater extent than in the past, persons working part-time, and less than year-round. In 1972, out of all males in the population aged 65 to 69, only 21 percent had worked year-round.

Not only does retirement become formalized in industrial society, where the realms of family and of work are separate; the retired are also separated from kin. I am not passing judgment on whether this is good or bad, for there is evidence that older people prefer to live on their own.[4] But as a problem it becomes separated out to stand on its own: it is no longer a problem specific to occupational life, nor is it a problem pertaining to family life. It becomes society's problem.

Further, the decreasing proportion of workers in the labor force is itself a result of "technological progress." As Sheppard points out, the post-World War II period in Western industrialized countries has witnessed the most rapid rate of exit from the labor force, due to the fact that with the phenomenal development of technology, an ever-decreasing number of man-hours are necessary for a rising level of income and a living standard that is deemed desirable.[5]

It is in the age category of the 55 to 64 year-old males that actual or planned retirement has undergone some marked change. From 1947 to 1973, the labor-force participation of men in this age group declined from 90 percent to 78 percent. Also, of employed women over age 62, many choose early retirement.

Early retirement is associated with several factors, among them marital status, health, and occupation. Those married are less likely to retire early than the single, widowed, or divorced. Poor health is also often given as a reason for early retirement. Occupation plays a large part as well.

In 1969, 90 percent of 58 to 63 year-old professionals were in the labor force, but only 83 percent of clerical workers; 84 percent of craftspeople were in the labor force, but only 79 percent of operatives and 73 percent of laborers were in the work force that year.[6]

It is worthy of note that educational level is not related in the same way to retirement intentions of men and women. Male prospective retirees tend to have less education than those not planning to retire, which is consistent with occupational differences. However, female prospective retirees are likely to have more education than women with no intention of retiring.

It seems to me that this contradictory finding can be explained by occupational differences as well. Men's educational level is usually matched by their occupations; it is those in routine occupations who are more likely to retire or to plan to do so. In contrast, women's educational level is usually not matched by the socio-economic level of their occupation. Women generally are likely to have routine occupations,[7] and those who are better educated tend to be dissatisfied with the relatively low level of employment available to them. Sheppard

found that in 1970-71, among Ford employees eligible for early
retirement, the lower-skilled retired before age 65 at a rate much
higher than the higher-skilled. Other studies, notably the one done by
Michigan's Survey Research Center, also showed that twice as many
blue-collar as white-collar workers want to retire if they have the
financial means for doing so.[8]

Generally, it can be said that the more alienating the work, the
more likely it is that the worker will want to retire if economic conditions permit. Since male workers with little education are likely to
have routine jobs, it is understandable that they would feel more
alienated than workers with more education and hence would want to
retire earlier than the latter. For women, in contrast to men, higher
education is not nearly as often associated with more highly skilled
work. Better-educated women would therefore be more frustrated in
jobs that require a relatively low level of skills, since they are likely to
feel that their education is not being rewarded. Therefore, the better-
educated women tend to behave like the less-educated men in their
wish to terminate alienated labor earlier than at the mandatory age.

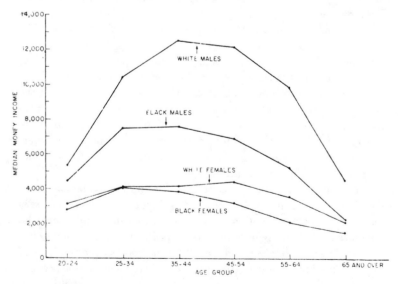

Figure 1 Median income of persons[a] by age, sex and race, 1973. (From Table 53,
U.S. Bureau of the Census (1975a).)

[a]Excludes persons without any income.

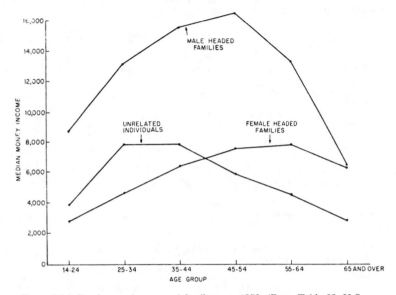

Figure 2 Median income by age and family type, 1972. (From Table 25, U.S. Bureau of the Census (1975a).)

Economic conditions are a real problem for older people. As you will see from Figures 1 and 2, aging has an equalizing effect. While after age 54 white males continue to have a great advantage over black males, and especially over both white and black females, the differences narrow with increasing age. We might call this a case of *negative equalization*. This phenomenon of negative equalization is discernible in all disadvantaged categories, as Figure 1 also shows. Women—and black women more so than white women—don't change their income much in the course of the life cycle: all *women* are comparatively equal, just as all *old* people are relatively equal.

As you will see from Table 1, over 70 percent of all single, widowed, or divorced males, and 82 to 87 percent of all single, widowed, or divorced females, whether they live in families or not,

Figure 1 and 2 are from James H. Sculz, ''Income Distribution and the Aging,'' in Handbook of Aging and the Social Sciences, Robert H. Binstock and Ethel Shanas, Eds., New York: Van Nostrand Reinhold Co., 1976, pp. 561–591.

TABLE 1:1973 TOTAL MONEY INCOME OF PERSONS 62 YEARS OLD
AND OVER BY MARITAL AND FAMILY STATUS.

| | | SINGLE, WIDOWED, OR DIVORCED | | | |
| | | MALES | | FEMALES | |
Income class	Married couples	In families	Not in families	In families	Not in families
Less than $3,000	11.3	51.4	45.6	73.4	57.3
3,000-4,999	22.4	19.3	25.6	14.3	24.3
5,000-9,000	35.6	18.1	17.5	9.6	14.1
10,00 or more	30.5	11.2	11.3	2.7	4.3
Total percent	100.0ᵃ	100.0	100.0	100.0	100.0

ᵃMay not add to 100 percent due to rounding.
SOURCE: Derived from Table 54, U.S. Bureau of the Census (1975a).

TABLE 2: 1973 TOTAL MONEY INCOME OF PERSONS 62 YEARS
OLD AND OVER, BY RACE.

| | MARIED COUPLES | | SINGLE, WIDOWED, OR DIVORCED | |
Income class	White	Black	White	Black
Less than $3,000	10.1	29.8	56.8	81.9
3,000-4,999	21.8	30.8	22.6	11.7
5,000-9,999	36.4	26.3	14.8	6.4
10,000 or more	31.8	13.0	6.0	.9
Total percent	100.0ᵃ	100.0ᵃ	100.0ᵃ	100.0ᵃ

ᵃMay not add to 100 due to rounding.
SOURCE: Derived from Table 54, U.S. Bureau of the Census (1975a).

made under $5,000 in 1973. The difference between whites and
blacks is greater yet, as Table 2 also shows. Poverty rates for men,
and for women as well, increase threefold with retirement after age 65
held constant (Table 3).

Over the past 20 years the unemployment rate of men in the
55-64 age category, in spite of the protection of seniority, has consistently been higher than the rates for the younger adult male
category. As for the "open-end" category of 65 and over, the male
unemployment rates since 1962 have consistently been greater than

the rates of those of age 55 to 64. This higher unemployment rate suggests that there is no guarantee of job tenure for older men who do not retire.[10]

Yet these statistics tell only part of the story. Unemployment of the aged cannot be understood from unemployment statistics alone. Two facts stand out: first, once unemployed, older workers remain unemployed longer. Secondly, the official method for measuring and defining unemployment omits what has been called "hidden unemployment" which comprises, among others, older persons who have not actively sought employment in a given period, although they had been looking for work prior to that period and would accept employment if offered.

Once unemployed, the older worker remains unemployed longer, is more likely to exhaust unemployment compensation benefits, becomes discouraged, and drops out of the labor force. The last stage in this process eliminates such persons from the counts of the unemployed.

Age *per se* is frequently a basis for not employing the older job applicant. In one study of 2,000 unemployed in Detroit in 1962, it was

TABLE 3: POVERTY RATES[a] AMONG AGED[b] FAMILIES AND UNRELATED INDIVIDUALS, BY WORK STATUS AND SEX, 1973.

| | PERCENT POOR | | | |
| | NOT RETIRED[c] | | RETIRED[d] | |
Family status	Men	Women	Men	Women
All 65 and over	4.9	10.9	15.5	33.6
Family head	4.2	*[e]	11.5	17.9
Unrelated individual	9.8	11.4	31.9	37.3

[a]Percent poor.
[b]Age 65 or older.
[c]Worked year-round, full time: data for part-year or part-time workers not shown.
[d]Head or unrelated individual did not work during the whole year.
[e]Percentage not computed for case less than 50,000.
SOURCE: Unpublished data provided by the Social Security Administration, derived from special Office of Economic Opportunity tabulations.

found[11] that age—even when such factors as education, sex, race, previous labor force experience, etc., were controlled—remained a significant factor in their job-seeking experience. In a study based on a group of men not usually in the "hard-core" population of the unemployed—engineers and scientists in the defense industries of the West Coast—it was found that even when measures of technical competence and education were held constant, age was the most significant variable explaining their layoffs. And among these unemployed engineers and scientists, duration of joblessness was a function of age: the older the professional, the longer he remained unemployed.[12]

If we remember that most employees' health-insurance benefits are tied to their employment, the loss of a job increases the probability of reduced health care, thus aggravating the part that illness plays in labor-force withdrawal. There is also some evidence that the expectation of unemployment and the actual layoff itself can increase the probabilities of selected psychosomatic illnesses. Unemployment itself then becomes a basis for illness which in turn serves as an obstacle to reemployment.[13]

Unemployment in old age for men cannot be considered without reference to the changes in the employment of women. From 1947 to 1973, women's participation in the work force increased at a rate of over 40 percent. In 1920, 20 percent of American women between the ages of 18 and 64 were in the labor force; this proportion increased to 30 percent in 1940 and 50 percent in 1970. By now, I believe the figure is 61 percent. What is important to our concern with aging is that in the past most women in the labor force were the young ones, the unmarried, or the young married ones without children. What has changed is that married women, age 35, even with small children and with husband present, have entered the labor force. In contrast to men, women have increased their participation in the labor force, and older women are not as likely to retire as are older men.

In the past, women's participation decreased after age 55. In 1960, after the increase in demand for female labor in the 1950's, it decreased from 33 percent in the 55 to 59 age range to 26 percent in the 70 and older category. Similarly, in 1970, women's participation in the labor force decreased from 38 percent at age 55 to 59 to 32 percent at age 70 and over. But for 1990 the projections are that the pro-

TABLE 4: AGED WOMEN WITH POVERTY
LEVEL INCOMES, 1973.

Marital status	BELOW POVERTY LEVEL	
	Number[a]	Percent
Married, husband present	375	8.3
Married, husband absent	29	*[b]
Widowed	1,578	24.9
Divorced	97	31.4
Separated	55	54.5
Never married	165	21.6

[a] Thousands.
[b] Base less than 75,000.
SOURCE: U.S. Bureau of the Census (1975b).

portion of women in the labor force at age 70 and older will be exactly
the same—41 percent—as their proportion of the 55 to 59 category.[14]

Yet women are poorer than men, and especially single women.
This may account for their greater reluctance to retire. "In our
society, at every age and every stage, women are more vulnerable to
poverty than men."[15] (Tables 1 and 3). As Figure 2 shows, the "unrelated" (i.e., mostly single women) experience a serious drop in income after age 55. Of this group the divorced and separated (Table 4)
constitute the highest proportion living in poverty. If we consider that
the divorce rate between 1968 and 1975 went up by about 35 percent
(for those 40 to 64, the rate went up one-half), the proportion of
women living in poverty must have increased accordingly.[16]

What is important to note is the change in the life cycle of
women (Figure 3). With fewer children, the average age of women at
the birth of the last child is 27. This means that childbearing has
become a specialized activity. In the past (Figure 4) the average age of
marriage marked a downward trend in labor-force participation
which continued all through life. However by 1966, the average age
at which the last child enters school marked the beginning of an
upward trend in women's work outside the home. The proportion of
women in the labor market is at its highest at the time when the last
child marries.[17]

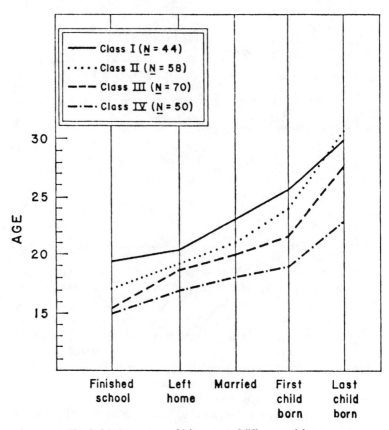

Fig. 3.-Median ages at which women of different social status reach successive events in the family cycle.

NOTE.-Women classified according to husband's occupation: Class I, business executives and professional persons; Class II, white-collar workers; Class III, blue-collar workers; Class IV, itinerant and unskilled workers.

In 1890, 13 percent of the women who worked were married; in 1959, 55 percent. As recently as 1940 only one out of 10 female workers had children at home under 18; by 1961, it was one out of three.

For men, the trend is to shorten the total number of years spent in the labor force, to be older than they used to be when they start to work, and younger when they retire. For most women, the trend is to extend the total number of years spent in the labor force.[18]

For the first time in American industrial society, women become defined as economic adults: that is, people who can take care of themselves and are indeed expected to take care of themselves. With the liberation that comes with equal or not-so-equal employment opportunities, comes the obligation to behave in the ideal pattern of the American individualist male who does it all by himself, without anybody's help. For if one woman out of three with children under age 18 is at work, the single women in the neighborhood, or those whose children have left the home, feel a moral obligation to work, in addition, of course, to economic need. When grandmothers are working, not even grandchildren are expected to look at them as people who need to be protected.

This leads me to say a few words about family relations. The relation between grandparents and grandchildren has changed in modern society, and especially the relation between grandmothers and their children's children. In a society in which tradition is important—in contrast to ours—grandparents' usefulness does not so much depend on their ability to produce as on their ability to pass on reminiscences to younger generations. The old only play an important part in assuring social continuity between the generations. But in a society of rapid technological and social change, the knowledge grandmothers can transmit is of little value compared with the new knowledge being acquired by the young. When new inventions are thought to be more important than historical events, when understanding the computer is considered more important than the myths, legends and experiences of the past, the value of grandparents is vastly diminished.

In my own fieldwork in a general hospital, older women did not even have with them a picture of a grandchild. In my three months of observation of and talk with elderly patients on a 25-patient ward, I encountered only one elderly woman who was able to produce a photograph of her grandchild. Other patients promised to ask their daughter or daughter-in-law to give them a picture of the grandchild

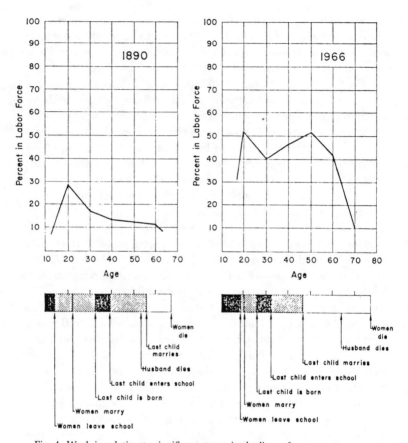

Fig. 4.-Work in relation to significant stages in the lives of women.

SOURCES: National Manpower Council, *Womanpower*. New York: Columbia University Press, 1957, p. 307. Right-hand portion of figure has been revised based on labor-force data taken from *1967 Manpower Report,* U.S. Department of Labor, Table A-2, p. 202, and on family cycle data taken from Glick, Heer, and Beresford, 1963, p. 12.

at their next visit, but usually forgot to do so. Health professionals—and no doubt other mediating agents as well—easily fall prey to the hostility that often develops between children and their parents. One daughter of an elderly patient told me, "The doctor didn't think it was good for my children to have their grandmother with them too often." When I was consultant at the adolescent unit at Harvard's Children's Hospital, a physician told me he agreed with the mother of his young patient that the child should be kept away from the grandparents (I am glad to report that I helped him change his opinion). There has occurred a general distancing of relationships between the generations; grown children with their own families don't need their parents much because they make it on their own. Reciprocally, grandparents, especially grandmothers, are themselves likely to work, and feel they have given enough years to caring for family members. They are relieved that their children are on their own!

As Bernice Neugarten and Karol Weinstein[19] have put it, it used to be that women described "a preparatory period" in which women "visualized themselves as grandmothers, often before their children were married. With the presently quickened pace of the family cycle, in which women experience the emptying of the nest, the marriages of their children, and the appearance of grandchildren at earlier points in their own lives, the expectation that grandmotherhood is a welcome and pleasurable event frequently seems to be accompanied also by doubts that one is indeed 'ready' to become a grandmother or by the feelings of being prematurely old . . . "

Twenty out of 70 grandmothers, and 19 out of 70 grandfathers, in Neugarten and Weinstein's research, felt "remote from their grandchildren." Most of the grandmothers said essentially, "It's great to be a grandmother, of course, but I don't have much time." Only three of the 70 men and eight of the 70 women said that they are resource persons for their grandchildren, as for example: "I take my grandson down to the factory and show how the business operates. . . . That's something his father can't do yet, although he'll do it for *his* grandchildren." The weakening of such serial reciprocity is also shown in a change of inheritance patterns: more and more in recent times people bequeath their belongings to strangers—neighbors, friends, or institutions rather than to their children—a trend which marks a gradual breakdown of serial reciprocity between the generations.[20]

The loss of the function of grandparenting is one aspect of increased isolation of the elderly. Let me note, however, that increased isolation of the aged is to be considered a trend, not an absolute fact. Most older men or women are in contact with their children who usually are on call in case of illness, and there are mutual visits, especially at ceremonial occasions. But older people need younger people more than the latter need them.

Even in the best of cases, as the one reported by Howard Webber, where a woman, Eleanor Vernor, is taken in by her daughter and son-in-law, who shower her with affection and consideration, the old lady senses the games that are being played to make her feel good; and in spite of all the support she gets from her children, there is little real closeness. She reports that life had become difficult when living alone: "The milkman had begun counting out the wrong change for me. The paper boy had delivered the newspaper or not, as the inclination struck him. And the clerks at the grocery store had amused themselves by playing petty tricks on me.... To keep me from insisting on justice and courtesy, they relied on the precariousness of an old person's reputation, on the skepticism with which the word of the old is regarded, on my fear and feebleness." She goes on to tell of the reassurances her children gave her, their little consideratenesses, but she considers them all "games." "Games," she says, "about who I am." She says that her children do not disappoint her, but "What has disappointed me is the way things are—the subtle conspiracy of my weakening nerves and tendons and of the alteration in my outward flesh and of my changing disposition that has cut me off from the continent of the young and put me on the ancient island where I am...."[21]

I have spoken in some detail about the economic aspects of old age and retirement. But the social aspects seem to be equally gripping. Take only what might be considered a side issue: the problem of free time. This becomes a major social psychological problem, not because people don't know how to spend their leisure time, but because they don't know how to spend it in the company of others. There is a discrepancy in the availability of time for oneself, as compared to those with whom one wants to associate. Take the relations between the generations. The younger generation has little free time, what with job and career building—today frequently two careers rather than one—and small children. A major problem of the aged is having too much free time.[22] Proportions of older people who say they do not know what to do with their time increase with age, and few complain about not having enough time, nor do they want more of it.[23] Free time is especially exasperating if the people one wants to associate with do not have any.

With the loss of a job, one loses associates on the job, not only because one ceases to have common experiences with them, but because their rhythm of life is no longer the same as one's own. Of course, loss of associates at work is an important aspect of retirement and old age—the rhythm of time being only one instance of discontinuity. One study found that the social aspects of the job were valued among all categories of employed persons, many respondents reporting that if they did not work they would miss the friends and associates at work.[24] There are, as noted earlier, occupational differences. In his study of industrial workers, Dubin[25] found that social interaction on the job is not necessarily very important to the individual. But if one distinguishes white collar employees and skilled factory workers from those who have routine jobs, it bears out that it is the latter who tend to be more withdrawn, with fewer friends, and less satisfactory family relationships than the skilled or white-collar workers.[26]

In our society, retirement usually reduces opportunity for social contacts. For men, and, I believe, increasingly for women, there is a sense that work is essential to their identity.

Everett Hughes has called attention to the importance of a person's work for the experience of self. He says: "A man's work is one of the most important parts of his social identity, of his self, indeed of his fate in the one life he has to live, for there is something almost as irrevocable about the choice of occupation as there is about choice of a mate." So much is this the case, Hughes suggests, that when you ask people what work they do, they are likely to answer in terms of "who they are." They attempt to establish and validate their own identity by referring to the identity of their work in a publicly recognized and preferably esteemed occupational or professional category.[27] People who lose a job have a sense of loss of identity, especially since social interaction with associates on the job decreases or discontinues altogether.

People who retire have a fourfold loss: their financial resources decrease sharply; their sense of identity suffers a blow; depending on their occupation, they may be deprived of an activity they cherished; and their loss of role is not only the loss of an activity, but the loss of relationships with others. Zena Blau states that it is not age nor physical changes so much as the loss of an occupation that "leads people to change their age identity and accept old age." In her research she found that only a small proportion of the employed in their sixties (18 percent) thought of themselves as old; but the retired of the same age felt old nearly as often as employed people of 70 years and beyond (37 percent and 41 percent respectively).[28]

Age is also accompanied by a diminishing rate of participation in voluntary associations, except for church membership; and even this does not tell us much about actual participation. Activity in church-related groups already begins to decline at an earlier age, but women are likelier than men to continue to attend church regularly and to join in other forms of religious events. Older people are more likely to be actively involved in associations if they are still working and married and if they are visiting with friends. Again, it is the retired people, men or women, and especially those who do not have a spouse, for whom there is a sharp drop in involvement in organizations associated with the occupation, although the decline is more noticable among men than among women, and is less true of the upper classes.[29]

The research done by Zena Blau in an urban community and in a small town confirms these general trends.[30] Yet there are social-structural factors that make for differences in the maintenance of friendships. In Blau's research it turned out that "only the participation of the married declines with age" whereas "that of the widowed does not." In her sample, widowhood had little effect on the social participation of people over age 70, but it had detrimental effects on the friendships of those who were still in their 60's.

These findings seem incongruous, especially since widowhood at an earlier age, rather than at a later age, should strike as more of a shock. Also, widowhood as well as retirement represents the loss of a major institutional role. Each "implies some changes in the extent and nature of the social activities among older people," and "it could be expected that. . . a change either in marital or employment status should have an adverse effect on friendships.''

To understand the paradoxical data we must remember the familiar fact that there are more widowed persons among older than among younger people. Trivial as this statement sounds, it provides a clue to the unexpected finding: ''Widowhood appears to have an adverse effect on social participation when it places an individual in a position different from that of most of his or her age and sex peers.'' The widowed person under age 70 is likely to be an ''odd person since most of the other people at social gatherings are probably still married and participate with their spouses. But after 70, it is *married couples* who are deviants if they continue to participate jointly in social activities since most of their friends in this group are likely to be widowed.''

The difference between men and women further confirms this analysis. Married men associate more with friends than married women; in contrast, when they are under age 70, widowers do so less than widows. Widowhood seems to be less detrimental to the partici- pation of women under 70 than to that of men in the same age category, because the woman in her 60's is more likely to have some associates who also are widowed. The younger widow is not in as socially deviant a position as the younger widower. Hence, widow- hood does not affect the participation of younger women to the same extent as that of younger men.

The effect that changes in major status have on the friendships of older people depends on the prevalence of these changes in the social structure. ''A change in status which places the individual in a deviant position in his or her age or sex group interferes with oppor- tunities to maintain old friendships. For if a change in a major status places an individual in a *minority* position among peers, it differenti- ates interests and experiences from theirs and thereby reduces the mutual bonds that serve as the basis for the formation and persistence of friendships. But if the same status change becomes *predominant* in a social group, then it is the individual who retains the earlier status who becomes the deviant, and consequently it is his or her social par- ticipation that suffers.''[30]

The effect of retirement seems to follow a similar pattern. As noted earlier, retirement at any age reduces or abolishes opportun- ities of contact with coworkers. But early retirement puts the retiring individual in a deviant position among associates, the majority of whom will still be working. The retired cannot share experiences with workers who are still on the job and whose conversations will reflect that fact, whether they brag about their achievements or complain about conflicts with supervisors.

Zena Blau observes,[30] "Retirement deprives the older individual of the run of common experience that is shared by people who work. As a result this person can no longer participate in the give-and-take of employed friends." As Blau further notes, "The retirant over 70 is less likely to encounter this problem because a good many of his friends are in the same position. Conversely, where retirement is more prevalent, it is the employed man over 70 who tends to occupy a deviant position with respect to his age and sex peers and consequently associates less with friends than his retired counterpart."

The same effect of early retirement does not seem to apply to women, at least not in Blau's study, done some 25 years ago. Where a woman's main role and involvement is in the family even if she is working, the focus of her social life is that of the household, or her children, or grandchildren. Hence the job or retirement is not as frequently a basis for the exchange of common experiences.

So far the emphasis has been on objective circumstances as well as on the behavior of the aged. And if it is in general correct to say that older people are more likely to withdraw to some extent from active participation with friends, or in organizations, or in seeking employment, this is probably correct on a broad superficial level. But we must be aware of the fact that older people are also given the message that they are not especially wanted. For example, there is some evidence that while church groups are willing passively to accept the participation of older people, few actively solicit it.[31] This is similar to the phenomenon reported by Sheppard and Belitsky, where the older the job-seeker, the fewer number of services (e.g., testing or counseling, referral to retraining programs or to employers for a job interview), on the average, were received from the Employment service. The importance of this kind of evidence of age discrimination can be inferred from the further finding that degree of job-finding success was related to the number of such services received from the employment service agency.[32]

As with employment, so with participation in organizations: older people have a tendency to withdraw. However, others—be they organizations or individuals—encourage them to do so. And as with employment, health or lack of it plays an important part in such withdrawal. But here also the effect is reciprocal. The discomfort of aches and pains is felt more strongly if one has time, and even more so if there is little encouragement from others to pull oneself together. One doesn't have to be seriously ill to decide to stay away from a meeting. Not feeling well or being tired is sufficient to substitute the television for going out.[33]

In our society not much is expected from the elderly. They are considered to have finished doing their duty by society and the next generation; they don't owe any contribution. Conversely, nothing is owed them. Nobody has any claim on them; they tend to be socially obsolete.[34]

I have said hardly anything about illness and health. But this audience would not expect from me any revelations on that subject. I shall therefore limit myself to a few points only.

Acute illness draws people together. Children will visit and help, and so will friends. But chronic illness drives people apart. A person who is ill for a long time finds his or her network thinning out, to the point when finally the old people find themselves in nursing homes. Most of the research that has been done about the social networks of the aged has omitted nursing homes because it is more difficult to get access. Visits of relatives (with the exception perhaps of the nearest ones) and of friends grow less and less frequent as time goes on. It has also been noted that patients who are visited by relatives or friends get more care and attention from staff[35]—a point which raises the issue of the cumulativeness of the effects of isolation.

As it is with health, so it is with mental health. The older people get, the more likely they are to be mentally impaired. As Table 5 shows, the Midtown Manhattan Study[36] in 1954 found that mental impairment rates went up from 7 percent to 14 percent, to 16 percent, and finally to 22 percent from decade to decade.

The Midtown Manhattan Study of Mental Illness was replicated 20 years later, and there is good news. It is with this that I want to end my address. While there still is an association between age and

Table 5:-General Mental Health Impaired Rates
in Decade-of-Birth Cohorts

	A + 1900 (N = 134)	B + 1910 (N = 199)	C + 1920 (N = 195)	D + 1930 (N = 167)
1954 Age, yr	50–59	40–49	30–39	20–29
Rate	22%	16%	14%	7%
1974 Age, yr	70–79	60–69	50–59	40–49
Rate	18%	12%	10%	8%
Difference	– 4% †	– 4% †	– 4% †	+ 1% †

*N = 695.
†Not statistically significant using the 1 test of differences between
correlated means.

Table 6 :-General Mental Health (GMH) Rates of impairment
By Generation-Separated Pairs of Like-Age Cohorts

Cohort A. * GMH I rate	22%
Cohort C. † GMH II rate	10%
Difference	– 12%
Significance	p <.01
Cohort B. ‡ GMH I rate	16%
Cohort D. § GMH II rate	8%
Difference	– 8%
Significance	p <.0511

*N = 134: age 50 to 59 years in 1954.
†N = 195: age 50 to 59 years in 1974.
‡N = 199: age 40 to 49 years in 1954.
§N = 167: age 40 to 49 years in 1974.
||Using two-sample 1 tests.

mental impairment, each cohort shows a marked decrease in
impairment as measured in that study. Although the differences are
not statistically significant, the trend is consistent for all four birth
cohorts.

But there is more. What *is* statistically significant are the differences between age categories. As one can make out from Table 5, and as summarized in Table 6, the Mental Health Impairment Rate decreased from 22 percent to 10 percent for the 50 to 59 between 1954 and 1974; and from 16 percent to 8 percent for the 40 to 49 age category.

These improvements seem to stem mainly from those in the rates for women (Table 7). It is worth noting that at the time of the first study, the rates for women were significantly higher than the rates for men—26 percent compared to 15 percent in the 50 to 59 age group, and 29 percent compared to 9 percent in the 40 to 49 age group. On the basis of what we know about the changes in the social roles of women, we would expect the impairment rates of women to go up during the next 20 years. Role conflicts as a result of status inconsistency on the job and in the culture would make this plausible. As is so often the case, however, what seems "expectable" is contradicted by the data. Twenty years later, in 1974, the rates for women approximate those of men. Not only are the changes statistically significant. More important, changes in mental health are matched on the General Physical Health Index as well (Table 8). Further, in response to the question whether "anything is worthwhile any more," which was meant to uncover latent suicidal tendencies, the

Table 7 :-General Mental Health (GMH) Rates of impairment
By Generation—Separated Pairs of Like-Aging Cohorts
And Gender Subgroups

	Men	Women
Cohort A. * GMH I rate	15%	26%
Cohort C. † GMH II rate	9%	11%
Difference	– 6%	– 15%
Significance	Not significant	p<.01
Cohort B. ‡ GMH I rate	9%	21%
Cohort D. § GMH II rate	9%	8%
Difference	0%	– 13%
Significance	Not significant	p<.02

*N = 134: age 50 to 59 years in 1954.
†N = 195: age 50 to 59 years in 1974.
‡N = 199: age 40 to 49 years in 1954.
§N = 167: age 40 to 49 years in 1974.

Table 8 :-'Fair-Poor' Frequencies of General Physical
Health (GPH) by Generation-Separated Pairs of Like-Age
Cohorts and Gender Subgroups.

	Men	Women
Cohort A. * GPH I rate	13%	34%
Cohort C. † GPH II rate	14%	18%
Difference	+1%	-16%
Significance	Not significant	p<.02
Cohort B. ‡ GPH I rate	16%	24%
Cohort D. § GPH II rate	11%	9%
Difference	-5%	-15%
Significance	Not significant	p<.01

*N = 134: age 50 to 59 years in 1954.
†N = 195: age 50 to 59 years in 1974.
‡N = 199: age 40 to 49 years in 1954.
§N = 167: age 40 to 49 in 1974.

Table 9:-'Nothing Worthwhile' (LSP) Frequencies for Women
(N = 401) by Generation—Separated Pairs of
Like-Age Cohorts

Cohort A. * LSP I rate	33%
Cohort C. † LSP II rate	16%
Difference	-17%
Significance	p<.01
Cohort B. ‡ LSP I rate	31%
Cohort D. § LSP II rate	19%
Difference	-12%
Significance	p<.05

*Age 50 to 59 years in 1954.
†Age 50 to 59 years in 1974.
‡Age 40 to 49 years in 1954.
§Age 40 to 49 years in 1974.

proportion of women age 50 to 59 who agreed with this statement
dropped from 33 percent to 16 percent for the 50 to 59 year olds, and
from 31 percent to 19 percent for the 40 to 49 age group (Tables 8 and
9).

Srole and Fischer[36] speculate that the changes between the older
and the newer generation of middle-aged and older people is due to
the changing culture surrounding these birth cohorts—from a
restricted Victorian to a more equalitarian upbringing of the young. I

think this explanation is oversimplified, since it would not apply to the improvements of the same cohorts as shown in Table 5. I think a change in the opportunity structure for women in the last 20 years would illuminate both sets of data. But my hypothesis also awaits the test of evidence.

It might just be that changes in the gender structure, together with the recent policy changes for retirement for women *and* men, promise small improvements in the opportunity structure for all.

I would like to end my address with this optimistic note. Things are not as they used to be—but sometimes they even get a little better.

DISCUSSION

Chaired by Dr. Rose Laub Coser, this panel included: Joseph S. Barbaro, C.S.W., Executive Director, Catholic Charities, Diocese of Rockville Centre; James E. Ramseur, M.A., Executive Director, Central Islip Psychiatric Center; and Isidore Shapiro, A.C.S.W., Commissioner, Nassau County Department of Mental Health.

Audience:

I'm interested in a remark you made, Dr. Coser, concerning the earlier retirement of men versus the later retirement of women. In my work as a school administrator, I deal with an older population, and it seems, at least in education, that men are burning out much sooner than women on the same job. I notice that a number of men get into psychological difficulties at around age 50.

Dr. Coser:

There is such contradictory data on this. I wonder what you mean by burning out?

Audience:

Men who just can't cope with job responsibilities and therefore wind up leaving the job earlier. Or, being on the job, but not being as effective as their female counterparts.

Dr. Coser:

Do you have an idea as to whether those men have been working at the job all their lives and the women only part-time?

Audience:

The men have probably been working a greater number of years, since they did not take time out for child-bearing.

Dr. Coser:

There is such a thing as burning out when you do something all the time. The more routine the activity, the faster you burn out. My hunch is that it would be the same for men and women, depending on the routine of the job and the intensity.

Mr. Shapiro:

If men have worked in some professional capacity over a long period of time, at around age 50 they are more conscious both of their assets and their limitations. I believe at that point you begin to experience a revival of some of the self-doubts you had in earlier years. I think that women, who may have had a period of time away from work, enter into the professional field with a greater enthusiasm, with a sense of newness.

The word "burnout" is used a great deal in the mental health field; if you keep working with disturbed people the consequence is that you really feel that you are being burned out. I think that that would also hold true in the educational profession. When you sense that you are not really meeting some of your standards or goals you become discouraged or depressed. As you become older you increasingly realize how difficult life is. But at least you have some self-understanding, and you have built up a sense of confidence when you are older, even though you become more realistic about limitations.

Dr. Coser:

There is something else that occurs to me, and that is the rhythm of a career. What are the main aspects of a person's career? Promotion is one, and your colleagues or social relations is the other.

By age 50 there is no promotion to hope for. As far as income is concerned, when children are college-age, most parents are at the peak of their earning power. Their income will not go any higher. That is one reason that many women start working again.

In general, it has been found that women have stronger affiliative needs than men, and are more gratified by affiliations than men. When a woman enters a career, often later on in life, she may find a great deal of gratification in her work and from association with her colleagues, even if there is no promotion or raise to be expected. But for the man the work and the promotion are most important for his self-image. These different forms of job gratification should be looked at when we want to find out what makes people retire.

Audience:

In general, what factors at a work site are important for a positive or a healthy sociological climate?

Mr. Barbaro:

It seems to me that what we are talking about is, where do we get our satisfaction? At one time it was thought that the major source of satisfaction was salary. However, more recent studies have shown that salary is about number five on the list. The prime satisfaction has to do with a feeling of achievement on a particular job. It seems to me that whether we are happy or unhappy on the job has to do with whether we enjoy performing the day-by-day operation.

Mr. Ramseur:

I think one has to raise the question, is management committed to a positive and healthy work climate? That is extremely important. We have known for at least 50 years what is necessary to solve our problems with regard to the handicapped; and I would place the older person, for purposes of discussion, in that category.

Dr. Coser:

The higher you are on the salary scale, the less likely it is that you are going to say that salary is the most important thing in your life. Somebody told me the other day that David Rockefeller made the statement that he doesn't really care about money; money doesn't matter. So, he doesn't care about money but he knows very well what his power is with it. A feeling of achievement indeed is very important, but sometimes a raise or a promotion is symbolic of that achievement. Even though everybody says we are highly effective, and even though we make enough money, we need some visible sign that symbolizes achievement—a raise tells us we are doing well. This feeling of doing well is very important, especially for many women who for years and years were told that all they could do was housework. Many women, as soon as they enter a career, all of a sudden are flying. They begin to believe they can achieve anything.

Mr. Shapiro:

I thought of one more thing regarding so-called burnout. At a certain point in one's life you appreciate the fact that there are limits to your own development, not your intellectual development, but you begin to realize that there are certain things you really don't know. You have an appreciation of limits. When you are younger, for instance, you feel you can do almost anything. When you move into the 40's and 50's you realize you are not going to become a physicist or an astronaut, if those were ideals you had when you were younger. You find out you are really only a human being, with circumscribed potentials, and that you must then deal with the issues in front of you.

Audience:

I am a nursing director and a student in a graduate program in gerontology. I am interested in what you said about the alienation of the generations and the changing role of the grandmother in particular. If a grandmother is out there active in the world and learning and doing, I would think there would be more respect, and that she would hold a new, and perhaps even improved position, in the family.

Dr. Coser:

I wasn't trying to say she would have no respect at all. I only say she wouldn't be needed as much, and nobody has a feeling that she has to be protected. Nobody today is going to get up in the subway and give a seat to an older woman or an older man. When I grew up the youngsters always got up for older people. They no longer do. I am not saying it is good or bad. But it is a sign of respect and it is also a sign of protecting somebody. You don't have to protect older people who work.

Today women who don't go back to work feel somehow that they are under more pressure. It used to be the other way around. I used to experience the opposite. There were the negative sanctions about working. Now the sanctions apply the other way. "You mean your kids are in college and you don't work? What are you doing with yourself?" The youngsters don't think you have a claim on them when you have a flat tire on the road. You can call AAA; you make your own money. The claim structure gets mixed up.

Mr. Shapiro:

I agree that there is an increasing detachment between generations. Our social systems have the elderly separated markedly from the general population in nursing homes or in villages where children aren't allowed. I don't have the solution, but it certainly is very troubling to see large numbers of elderly people together where the atmosphere is extremely subdued, in contrast to the hum where you have a mix of all ages. There is something in our whole cultural development in this country that creates this distancing between generations and I think this is tragic.

Mr. Barbaro:

In a community like ours, the role of the grandparents is not only changing, it is almost disappearing. There is a real exodus of mature people from this community. So children grow up thinking of grandparents as people to visit for a couple of weeks in the summer because they live in Florida, rather than people who are available to you all the time. That not only changes this relationship, it affects how the next generation of children are going to see grandparents. I am concerned that what used to be a close three-generation kind of household rarely exists now and is becoming further apart as time goes by.

Audience:

I believe a number of grandparents are not moving out of the mainstream. With a number of women returning to the work force there is a renewed role for and an interest in the function of grandparents. They come out to the house in the suburbs and often act as surrogate parents to relieve some of the pressures on the nuclear family. I think this is in the interests of everybody in the family.

Dr. Coser:

Possibly not always in the best interests of the grandmother. If she works she really has no time to help her daughter.

Audience:

The older woman is in a Catch-22 situation. She is most likely to be living below the poverty level. When she tries to become employed or stay employed, she is contributing to the breakdown of the family system that may help her when she gets to the point where she no longer can be employed.

Dr. Coser:

When she is available, her grandchildren really don't need her much any more, because they are already in college. The whole cycle of life has changed. When the grandmother retires and can really be a grandmother, her grandchildren are too old for her stories. The time for telling about your own life is already past.

Audience:

Are you taking an advocacy position for grandmothers staying in a grandmotherly role?

Dr. Coser:

I am not so sure older people want to be with younger people. I think it would be healthier if the groups were more mixed. A survey shows that as people grow older they prefer to be among older people rather than with their children. So I should not advocate that they do something they don't want. It is a change. I don't know if it is for good or ill.

Mr. Shapiro:

I think there is a changing concept. In the past, you had social institutions which encouraged the relationship between children and grandparents, and that also includes grandfathers, you know, not just grandmothers. Then, as opposed to the current trend, the connection between families existed in a social atmosphere; now that is breaking apart because of this country's changing economy. Because the social connections are failing, there is a greater demand on psychological connections, and what is emerging is the revelation that people *don't* have psychological connections with each other.

Mr. Barbaro:

We all agree that women in general outlive men. It seems to me that that separation, however, comes at a later age now than it did before. My mother was widowed when she was in her late 40's but now it happens to women in their 60's and 70's. So even after retirement, there is a larger group of retired people who for a period of time are together and therefore have an opportunity to pursue their common retirement plans.

We keep referring to the lone grandmother who is needed or dependent. From where we sit I see a lot more retired couples now pursuing their common interests and goals. How does this change that whole relationship between the three generations?

Dr. Coser:

It used to be that the death of the husband occurred, more or less on the average, shortly after the marriage of the first child. Now, the death of the husband comes some 10 or 15 years after the marriage of the first child, so that there are many more years for a man and woman to live together.

People talk about the frequency of divorce today, but they don't realize that people are married for much longer than was formerly the case. So, indeed, I agree with you. Life together is of much longer duration than it used to be.

Mr. Shapiro:

This talk of people being married longer reminds me of a story. In the 1960's Rockefeller had a symposium for senior citizens. The guest speaker was Harry Hirschfield who was then about 80. He was asked: "You have been married for 50 years, have you ever thought about divorce?" He said, "Divorce, never, but murder, many times."

Mr. Ramseur:

At an assembly of Gray Panthers in New York City about 5 years ago one of the Gray Panthers said, and I quote: "One's integrity and social place are closely bound with the presence or absence of an occupational status."

Audience:

Considering the general economic condition of American society today, how about the problems that confront us when we have increasing numbers of new persons entering the work force?

We have fewer jobs, and we have greater demands being made to retain people in the work force for longer periods of time, and also to offer opportunities to older women who are returning to the work force. One hears about employers who say that they must have room to provide promotional opportunities for the younger worker.

Dr. Coser:

The age of completion of education has been rising. This keeps some young people out of the work force who are not looking for a job. It would help in more ways than one if women were not paid so much less than men for an equivalent job. Do you have in mind the competition between men and women?

Audience:

I have more in mind the competition between the older and the younger.

Dr. Coser:

I don't have the answer, but I can suggest how to look at it. You have to look at the demography. We had a baby boom that started in 1947 and continued to 1963. The last of these babies are now finishing high school. We hear a hue and cry about lower attendance at college, and, of course, in high schools, as well. We don't need any more teachers; the whole field of education as a profession is going down. Then of course, when teachers are no longer needed, you say, why don't you let the young ones in and let the old ones go. But the problem is, in the 1950's, because of the baby boom, we needed nursery school teachers, elementary school teachers, nurses, and social workers to take care of all these children. That made for more and more teachers, and now that we have such a surplus of teachers who are getting old, we tell them, go.

That is how I would approach the problem in terms of the demography. We now have too many teachers. We have too many everything. But, teaching is something that is very visible; that is why I give this as an example.

We have never been able to plan, although we talk about planning all the time. We knew that the birthrate was going to go down, and we kept adding on careers and education. The point is that it was women who were trained for these baby-boom jobs.

A woman would come to a counseling service and say, "I want to be a lawyer," and the counselor would say, "Why do you want to be a lawyer, why don't you teach?" Well, all the women were directed into one field; and now they are upset, and rightly so.

Another problem is the competition between men and women. Actually there is not much competition in the real sense of the word. There is segregation of jobs. We have a dual-labor market. Women go one way, men go the other. That is true also for training in industry. The personnel director sees a woman and a man coming and says, you go over there and you go the other way for training. How does the personnel director make an assessment? This one is a woman and that one is a man. You don't invest much in the training of a woman. Right? So, then the women do one kind of job, but it is poorly paid. So they think after a while, better I go home and paint my kitchen walls instead of doing this unskilled job, there is no pro-motion anyway. Then the employer says, see, I told you so, women won't stay at their jobs, that is why we don't train them.

We have a dual-labor market and, if that continues, women are going to make less and less, and they are therefore going to have to stay more and more on the job when they get old. They can't retire even if they want to because they are not making enough. So it is really no use to talk about equal pay for equal work. Because if all truck drivers who are men make the same, and all nurses who are women make the same, the latter still make less although it's the same pay for the same job.

Men are attendants and women are aides. Then you can give them a different wage, right? Men who are truck drivers have an average education of 10 years' schooling, but many highly educated women are doing routine work. So the whole problem of competition is—what do you compete for? Women and men do not compete for truck drivers' jobs or for nursing jobs or for social workers' jobs or for teachers' jobs. What is equal pay is the low salaries of the women and the low salaries of the older men and women. It is a very complex problem.

Mr. Barbaro:

We have to keep in mind that we have a very high number of young adults who need jobs. Also, an employer can hire a younger worker at a lower salary. It seems to me that there is going to be continual tension until something happens in the job market. Certainly we shouldn't make the automatic assumption that the way to solve the problem is just to eliminate people who get older. We have to address full employment across the nation in all categories.

Mr. Shapiro:

A personal attitude I have had for a long time is that I prefer older people. There is a maturity that people achieve that can come only through living and learning. It has always puzzled me why many employers reject the older person as not employable. Some of the reasons that are given—the pension, more money—I don't think are the true reasons. Possibly we are rejecting something in ourselves.

Mr. Ramseur:

I come back to my very first comment: are we committed? We certainly have the talent, because if we can get to the moon and if we can provide weapons to destroy people, rather than helping people, we certainly have the wherewithal. The question has to be, are we committed?

Dr. Coser:

It is easier to destroy. It is easier to bulldoze a whole hospital than to change something in the wards. We all know that. We are all committed to the idea, and it is still not easy to put into practice, because we are dealing with people, with social structure. It is easier to get to the moon than it is to change the way people relate to each other in various stages of their lives, with different dispositions, roles, and interests. So it is not really an easy matter. Commitment in itself is absolutely necessary. It is a *sine qua non*. Without it, without commitment, we are not going to do anything. But once we are committed, let us not minimize the obstacles we are going to encounter. Commitment is a necessary, but not a sufficient, condition.

Audience:

If you want affirmative action for the aging you are going to have to legislate it just the way you had to legislate for minorities and for women.

Dr. Coser:

I am in favor of affirmative action, always have been, and hope to continue to do more for affirmative action of various types. I don't think we should give up. I think we should try and work in the direction you point out even if we don't get many results. I also think we should do that with due humility, because affirmative action has really not done much. Women in the universities are still in the same position they were at the beginning, by and large. That doesn't mean that the fight was in vain. That doesn't mean we shouldn't continue. We should; and commitment, indeed, is the answer here. But just by having a lobby, or by this gimmick or that, we are not really going to get at some basic social facts.

Audience:

With the changing life styles today and with people deferring marriage or in many cases not marrying at all, isn't a larger portion of spendable income in the hands of single people today? We know that the media and other forces in this society cater to people with spendable income. They certainly don't cater to older people.

Mr. Shapiro:

There seems to be a sort of tension or antagonism developing between groups. We talk about the aged and the young as if there is some mutual animosity evolving, maybe out of competition for jobs. People don't die as young as they used to; they remain on the job longer, and block the upward movement of the younger people. The tension is aggravated by lobbying efforts where you get certain benefits which are beneficial to the aged but are harmful, at least in their perception, to the young. I don't know if we ever get away from that kind of sociological tension. It is a realistic factor.

Audience:

Who do you feel are more reliable employees—the younger ones or the older ones? There is a very real tension and rivalry springing up between the old and the young. It is very apparent. The young workers see their Social Security tax deductions going up and up. They can't afford houses. They haven't got the money for their own families. They wonder where it is going to end. It is a fight between two groups. One is saying we need more, and the other is saying we can't give any more.

Dr. Coser:

I say there is never one answer to something. You ask who is more reliable, the young or the old? I guess you have in mind that the young workers are more reliable than the old ones. I don't think so.

Audience:

Just the opposite.

Dr. Coser:

Then you say the older ones are more reliable than the young ones. I don't think so either. The young ones will be more reliable in the sense that perhaps they will be sick less often. Perhaps. But then the young ones want to try and get ahead—they should want to—and change jobs faster. And the older one says, I really don't have to change jobs because my kids are already out of school and where am I going anyway? So the liability works both ways. But the most important thing I want to say is if we make statements that one part of the population, one type of people, is more this or less that, we make self-fulfilling prophesies.

Mr. Ramseur:

I don't think we can make generalizations as to whether any one population is more reliable than the other as far as employment is concerned. I would like to make an observation about compensation and money. About 18 months ago, I was fortunate enough to be asked whether I would like to have a foster-grandparents' program at my facility. I have a very active 35-bed adolescent unit that requires all the help we can get, and I was most delighted to welcome them. They came, both men and women, and began to work in the adolescent unit. Don't ask me to do a Ph.D. dissertation to defend it scientifically, but I would say to you, with respect and with humility, that they have moved youngsters that my professional staff could not move. The youngsters respect them. The foster grandparents give me the impression that they look forward to being with us as much as they did in their regular employment, and our adolescents look forward to their visits. On one occasion when one volunteer was not able to make it because of a transportation problem, the kids began to ask questions like, don't we have vehicles? I think that is a significant sign: a better sign than some of the textbooks give us.

Audience:

If, in fact, there is rivalry between the young and the old, then we must have an educational program that will help people to understand that if older people are kept in working positions they are going to be contributing to Social Security and not collecting it.

There is a kind of ridiculous Catch-22 in regard to discrimination. After taking a course in personnel management, I learned that I have to be very careful about applications. I went back and made very sure that my applications were really appropriate—they didn't ask age, race, marital status, or the number of children. Then I took another course, "Industrial Gerontology," and was told that if you don't ask the age of the person then you can't prove that you are not discriminating by reason of age. I think that many people who have really good intentions are often caught up in this type of frustrating ambivalence.

Mr. Barbaro:

We have the same problem with color. We don't ask about color and then we are asked by the Federal government what percentage of minorities we hire.

Dr. Coser:

I want to answer this question as a sociologist. I am in favor of getting all the data so that then we can analyze them. We will never have good social science unless we have the data.

Audience:

I believe that the conflict between the young and the old is not a new phenomenon. It is not brought on by Social Security. I remember reading in Cicero about the conflict between the old and the young, and I suppose that 2,000 years from now, generations to come will be discussing the same thing. It is a problem that will always exist.

Dr. Coser:

It is not always all for the worse. I am not so sure older people were so much happier when they were completely dependent on their children to support them. I don't think they were so much better off. The idea that we all had this extended family around, and everybody was loving everybody is a very exaggerated one. First of all, they weren't loving everybody. Second of all, there was never an extended family in this country, and not in England. In some other countries there were; in Italy, for example, it was more common. It depends on the country. We haven't had extended families ever since the founding of the Union. The nostalgic notion that every household has a grandmother is obviously demographically impossible. If a grandmother had five children—and lived long enough to have grandchildren which often she didn't—she couldn't possibly live with five children.

Of course, things were different because people were available to each other. They lived in a close neighborhood. They didn't live 3,000 miles apart. But not everybody today lives that far apart from relatives either. I am not so sure that it was all that much better, and that Social Security is worse than depending on children.

Mr. Shapiro:

I would like to add that these extended families brought family therapy into being, because of all the fighting and manipulation that went on in the family. We have a tendency in this country to idealize everything, and we all have a sort of secret idealization of the perfect family. Even in this discussion, we are trying to say that if we had certain things we would all realize the ultimate ideal—that we would always be happy and have perfect loving parents and loving children. You know, and I know, that that isn't true.

AUDIENCE:

I'd like to make a comment on lobbies and the power to obtain funds. We must accept the fact that there has to be a limit to the amount of money you are going to have. I'll use that pitcher of water on the dais as an illustration. There are just so many drops of water in that pitcher. If we all decide to have a drink, we will all have a little bit less. If a few of us decide that we need more than the others, somebody is going to go thirsty.

Audience:

We are here dealing with a natural phenomenon, and that is survival. Every one of you here is concerned with it. You are concerned with the particular value judgment that you hold dear and you will fight for its survival. Darwin said it best: Those who are well-equipped by nature are going to survive. Those who don't will have to fall by the wayside.

Dr. Coser:

We have spoken about many things. We have spoken about burning out on the job. We have spoken about grandmothers and grandfathers. We have spoken about the changed life cycle. We have spoken about affirmative action and lobbying. I think we have pinpointed certain problems. There is one other problem I want to bring up briefly. I know relatively little about it, but it seems to me that the problem of housing is a very important one. As somebody said, it touches the young and it touches the old. Perhaps this is a problem in which we can get consensus, where we don't have to divide and polarize people and say, the interests of the older are so different from the interests of the young. Perhaps there are a number of interests that men and women have in common, and the old and young have in common. I think the problem of housing is one of them.

Mr. Shapiro:

Referring back to the beginning of our discussion, there was a comment made about the elderly moving into separate communities.

If we had housing where the elderly could live in an open community and could maintain themselves in a reasonable style of living, I think that would be the healthiest evolution. Any ghetto-ization of any group is deadly.

Audience:

I know of a community where zoning was not permitted before there was a ruling that there would be no children in the development, because the community felt it couldn't support the additional taxes for the schools. So that immediately set the age. When I go there to see my father and I step out of the car, it is so quiet and so isolated.

Dr. Coser:

It is very shortsighted on anyone's part to say, this other sector does not concern me. I don't want to pay taxes for schools because I don't have children. The whole population profits from having an educated population. If I step out of my house and I go to the post office, or the bank, or the grocery store, or if I talk to a cab driver, I am going to be served better and I am going to be better off if that other person is educated. I am going to profit from good education whether or not I have children.

I think the same is true for the aged. The community will profit if the aged are in comfort, if they are not in demeaning positions. A community suffers if it has a ghetto of people who are miserable, unhappy. The stores can't flourish, business can't flourish, the schools can't flourish, the whole community is going to go to pieces. We cannot afford to say, I am not going to pay Social Security for other people; I am not going to pay school taxes for other people. I think what we do for other people we do for the whole community. The integration that you were talking about is dependent on society, and we are all dependent upon it.

REFERENCES

1. Cf. Arensberg, C.M., & Kinball, S.T. Family and Community in Ireland. In R.L. Coser, (Ed.), *The Family, Its Structures and Functions,*

New York: St. Martin's Press, 1974, 412-429.

2. Goody, J. Aging in Nonindustrial Societies. In Robert H. Binstock & E. Shanas, (Eds.), *Handbook of Aging and the Social Sciences.* New York: Van Nostrand Reinhold Co., 1976, 117-129.

3. Sheppard, H.L. Work and Retirement. In *Handbook of Aging and the Social Sciences. H. Binstock and Ethel Shanas, New York: Van Nostrand, 1976, 561-91.*

   Pampel, F.C. Changes in Labor Force Participation and Income of the Aged in the U.S., 1947-1976. In *Social Problems,* Dec. 1979, *27*, 125-142.

4. Bane, M.J. *Here to Stay: American Families in the Twentieth Century,* New York: Basic Books, 1976. Ch. 3.

5. Sheppard, *op. cit.*

6. Sheppard, *op. cit.*

7. Coser, R.L., & Rokoff, G. Women in the Occupational World: Social Disruption and Conflict. *Social Problems,* Spring 1971, *18*, 535-554.

8. Sheppard, *op. cit.*

9. Schulz, J.H. Income Distribution and the Aging. In *Handbook, op. cit.,* 561-91.

10. Sheppard, *op. cit.*

11. Wachtel, H. Hard-core unemployment in Detroit: Causes and Remedies. *Proceedings of 18th Annual Meeting of Industrial Relations Research Association, 1965,* Madison, Wisconsin: Industrial Relations Research Association, 1966, 233-41; Quoted by Sheppard, *op. cit.*

12. Loomba, R.P. *A Study of the Re-employment and Unemployment Experiences of Scientists and Engineers Laid Off from 62 Aerospace and Electronics Firms in the San Francisco Bay Area during 1962-63.* Center for Inter-disciplinary Studies, San Jose State College. Report Manpower Administration, U.S. Department of Labor (no date). Quoted by Sheppard, *op. cit.*

13. *Ibid.*

14. Sheppard, *op. cit.*

15. Schulz, *op cit.*

16. Glick, P.C. Demographic Changes in the Family. Paper presented at the National Conference on Work and Family, Happauge, New York, April 1978.

17. Neugarten, B.L. & Moore, J.W. The Changing Age-Status System. In B.L. Neugarten, (Ed.), *Middle Age and Aging.* Chicago: University of Chicago Press, 1968, 5-21.

18. *Ibid.*

19. Neugarten, B.L. & Weinstein, K.K. The Changing American Grand-parent. In *Middle Age and Aging, op. cit.,* 280-285.

20. Rosenfeld, J.P. *The Legacy of Aging.* Norwood, New Jersey: Ablex Publishing Co., *passim.*

21. Webber, H. Games. *The New Yorker,* March 30, 1963, reprinted in B.L. Neugarten, *Middle Age and Aging.* Chicago: University of Chicago Press, 1968, 423-427.

22. Kleemeier, R.W. (Ed). *Aging and Leisure.* New York: Oxford University Press, 1961.

23. Riley, M.W. & Foner, A. Inventory of Research Findings. *Aging and Society* (Vol. I). New York: Russell Sage Foundation, 1968.

24. Sofer, C. *Men in Mid-Career. Quoted by M.F. Lowenthal & B. Robinson. Social Networks and Isolation. In Handbook, op. cit.,* 433-456.

25. Dubin, R. Industrial Workers' Words: A Study of the Central Life Interests of Industrial Workers. *Social Problems,* (1956), *3,* 131-42.

26. Kornhauser, A. *Mental Health of the Industrial Worker,* New York: John Wiley, 1965. Quoted by Lowenthal and Robinson, *op. cit.*

27. Hughes, E.C. *Men and Their Work.* New York: The Free Press, 1958, 43.

28. Blau, Z.S. *Old Age in a Changing Society,* New York: New Viewpoints, 1973, 104-105.

29. Lowenthal & Robinson, *ibid.*

30. Blau, Z.S. Structural Constraints on Friendships in Old Age. *American Sociological Review,* 1961, *26,* 429-39.

31. Atchley, R. C. *The Social Forces in Later Life,* Belmont, Cal.: Wadsworth, 1972, quoted by Lowenthal and Robinson, *op. cit.*

32. Sheppard, H.L. & Belitsky, A.H. *The Job Hunt,* Baltimore: The Johns Hopkins Press, 1966, quoted by *Sheppard, op. cit.*

33. Lowenthal, M.F. Social Isolation and Mental Illness in Old Age. *American Sociological Review,* 1964, *29,* 54-70.

34. Blauner, R. Death and the Social Structure. *Psychiatry,* November, 1966, *29,* 378-94.

35. Glaser, B. & Strauss, A.L. *Time for Dying,* Chicago: Aldine, 1968.

36. Srole, L. & Fischer, A.K. The Midtown Manhattan Longitudinal Study vs. 'The Mental Paradise Lost' Doctrine. *Archives of General Psychiatry,* Feb. 1980, *37,* 209-220.

INDEX

DATE DUE

JUN 30 '96			